The Mouse That Roars

KAREN WILLIAMS

Copyright © Karen Williams 2015

The moral right of Karen Williams to be identified as the author of this work has been asserted by her in accordance with the Copyright, Designs and Patents Act 1988. All Rights reserved. No part of this book may be reproduced, stored in a retrieval system, or transmitted, in any form or by any means, electronic, mechanical, photocopying, recording or otherwise, without the prior written permission of the copyright owner.

ISBN 978-1-849148-58-0

Art by Kingsley Nebechi

Acknowledgements

I'd like to thank everyone who has been part of my life and impacted on the person I am today, including those who have taught me valuable lessons! This book is for my family, friends, colleagues, clients, and anyone who finds this book inspiring.

This book wouldn't have happened without support from my good friend, Esther Harris, who challenged me to go deeper than I really wanted to, and helped me to create this book in the form that it is today.

But most importantly I dedicate this book to my Dad, without whom it would never have been finished.

Kenneth Ronald Legg, my Dad, my inspiration
25 June 1943 – 23 May 2013

Contents

Prologue – A letter to my younger self — 1

Chapter 1 – Being the mouse that roars — 5

Chapter 2 – Love over checkout number 25 — 9

Chapter 3 – Becoming a star — 13

Chapter 4 – The light bulb moment — 19

Chapter 5 – Becoming a life coach — 35

Chapter 6 – Anything is possible — 45

Chapter 7 – Getting in touch with my why — 51

Chapter 8 – Just feel the fear and... — 60

Chapter 9 – Taking one step at a time — 71

Chapter 10 – Modelling excellence — 79

Chapter 11 – The difference that makes the difference — 89

Chapter 12 – How to write a book — 99

Chapter 13 – What the mind can conceive, it can achieve — 109

Chapter 14 – It's time to stand out — 117

Chapter 15 – What if I had a year to live?	12
Chapter 16 – My bucket list	13
Chapter 17 – Doing the things that scare you	13
Chapter 18 – Living in the moment	15
Chapter 19 – Not having a year to live	16
Chapter 20 – Managing your mojo	17
Chapter 21 – Topping up my vitality bucket	18
Chapter 22 – Leaving a legacy	18
Chapter 23 – The next steps in the journey	19
Epilogue – A letter to my older self	20
About Karen Williams	20

Prologue – A letter to my younger self

Dear Karen,

Weren't you a little mouse? Your mum remembers you as extremely timid: not wanting to talk to others, and happy in your own little world. You wouldn't pick up the phone, answer the door, and talking to others was an incredible stretch. You had a few close friends, and preferred to be with people you knew well rather than mixing with large groups.

As a four-year-old girl you suffered from glue ear; your middle ear was blocked and you struggled to hear. It was only after you had speech therapy that this was diagnosed, when you were unable to repeat back what was said because you didn't hear it right. You were in hospital three times for surgery to have grommets inserted, but it was having your tonsils out that finally cured it. You could be bribed into going to hospital with a Tiny Tears doll and a Bucks Fizz single but you felt frightened, vulnerable, different.

Despite this, your childhood was largely happy, as an only child with two loving parents. Raised in leafy middle class suburbia in the 1980s, life was simpler

The mouse that roars

back then. Communities were close-knit, it felt safe to play in the streets, and the biggest challenge you had was recording the Top 40 charts on a Sunday afternoon, and pausing the cassette before the DJ started to talk.

Your mum stayed at home, so was always there for you when you got home from school until you could look after yourself, and your dad worked his way up through the ranks at Lloyds Bank to become a manager. Your dad was a very reserved man, quiet and unassuming, whereas your mum was more outgoing. She was also the one who let you get away with things, whereas your dad was stricter with your upbringing.

But it didn't take much for the mouse to resurface. Your one attempt at tap dancing was disastrous when the teacher shouted at you and you fled the room in floods of tears. Naturally reflective, you were cautious, sensitive and introverted, and didn't cope with such direct feedback.

Moving to a new secondary school was a challenge and this was the start of a difficult period for you as a teenager. The last thing you wanted was to attract attention to yourself. But by the time you turned 14 you were tall for your age, were bigger than many of

A letter to my younger self

your classmates, and you wore thick-framed glasses. This made you feel that you stood out, and for all the wrong reasons. Children can be cruel, and you were singled out for your shyness and bullied by your classmates. The mouse was an easy target – but you had a quiet determination and an inner roar and there were times when you should have walked away from a confrontation but didn't...

Your parents got you help to get through it, and you managed to survive. Nine GCSEs and two A levels later you left school and were on the next stage of your journey. **And that's all that counts – the next stage.**

If I could spend time with you now as my younger self, I'd tell you not to worry. There are advantages to being quiet, and it didn't stop you from getting on in life or doing well at work when you got older. Actually the memories you have will help you to grow rather than constrain you. Maybe you weren't the lion you always wanted to be but you didn't let the mouse stop you. You learnt that there were ways that you could use these strengths to your advantage, which you can share with others now.

Lots of love, the older (and slightly wiser!) me xxxx

The mouse that roars

Chapter 1
Being the mouse that roars

The benefits of hindsight...! If I'd had a chance to speak to my younger self, this would have changed my life. Although I also believe that we need to face some difficult experiences to make us stronger, so we can teach others the lessons that we've learnt.

When I went through my personal struggles as a shy youngster, I could never have imagined that I'd be sharing my story with you and teaching people about courage and mindset, and helping other people to find their voice through writing their own books. I never thought I'd be a coach, a speaker, an author, an entrepreneur. And if you're wondering what happened next, then you'll just have to read on.

If you are or have ever been a mouse, are an introvert, feel like you're not heard, or if life seems too much and too scary, then this is your time to roar.

This book is part memoir, part self-help, and I'll be sharing my story and strategies that will help you if you are a shy person who feels that you have a bigger message to share with the world. You'll want to read on if you'd like some tips to create a more meaningful life. If you are fed up with feeling that your shyness is holding you back, let me share with you more about my experiences and advice to help.

Even if you're not an introvert and sometimes feel that life is passing you by, read on. You can also pass this book on to people who are on the planet to make a difference, and need a gentle nudge to make their big dreams happen.

Through this book I want to inspire you to be your best. It's not just another self-help book, nor is it a rags to riches business story. It's one where I'll be giving you real life examples, sharing with you things that have (and haven't!) worked for me, teaching you life lessons, and inspiring you to take action now.

It's not been easy writing this book. It has been my passion and my nemesis. It has been reincarnated many times as I've struggled to get across the message that I know needs to be out there. You might find that you are compelled to find out what's next or perhaps you'd prefer to dip in and out as you find things interesting. My job is to inspire and educate.

Being the mouse that roars

I also believe that the past doesn't have to equal the future, so what do you need to do to roar? In the next chapter, I'll take you back to my story.

The mouse that roars

Chapter 2
Love over checkout number 25

My parents always encouraged me to make the most of myself, despite my shyness. Like many youngsters, I didn't have a clue what I wanted to do when I left school, and leaving with two A levels, I didn't get the grades I needed to study tourism at university, which had been one of my dreams. To be honest, the thought of that was too daunting anyway. Why would I, the mouse, want to go into an environment where there were thousands of people jostling for attention? I didn't want to be out of my depth, so I opted for the safest choice.

Staying at home with my parents was easy, as was attending my local college where I studied for a BTEC HND in Hotel Management, although admittedly this still took me out of my comfort zone. With a Saturday job at my local supermarket, I started to develop into the person I am today.

The mouse that roars

In the summer of 1992, something else changed in my life, which kept me close to home. I fell in love!

I sometimes wonder how I found love wearing a particularly unflattering A-line dress in a burnt orange colour whilst working at Sainsbury's, although the guys in the chocolate brown uniform didn't look much better!

I'd already started dating at that stage, and like many young girls, I liked to gossip and chat with my girlfriends during lunch breaks. There was a lad at work, Peter, who had attracted my attention, and after confiding in two of my friends that I fancied him, they threatened to tell him unless I asked him out. However, I'm glad of it now and I'm still friends with one of those ladies today.

Now being a mouse, how did I approach this situation? I wasn't the type of girl who was brazen and brash, and I certainly didn't like to be rejected. But despite being quiet, I didn't let this stand in my way – although I wouldn't have done something without the intervention of my friends!

Love over checkout number 25

So I did it the mouse way. One Saturday evening as I left work while he was still working, I snuck up to checkout number 25, popped a note in his pocket, and quietly slipped away. In the note I asked him out and gave him my telephone number. I returned home, worried about what he might think, and whether he'd ever call me. And what if I returned to work the following week and he blanked me or even made fun of me?

But luckily the feeling was mutual, and two mice came together as one. Our second date was particularly memorable. One Thursday afternoon before his shift at work we went to the cinema. This was before the days of huge multiplexes, and we were the only people in the screening. The usher said "Two for sex and violence" as we went to see Basic Instinct, hardly the most romantic film! But afterwards, he gave me a present of a mixer cassette tape of romantic love songs, and we had our first kiss in the car park behind the cinema!

After quite a few dates, getting a home together, and many many years had passed, that boy, Peter Williams, finally became my husband.

Shy girl tip – Do something that scares you

Being a shy girl (or boy) doesn't mean that you can't do things that scare you; you just might have a different way of doing something. You shouldn't feel bullied into doing things, but if it's something that might give you an advantage, how can you do it in a way that feels comfortable to you?

Just because something feels tough shouldn't stop you from doing it. If you never take a step out of your comfort zone, you'll never do what you really want to do or achieve the things that you've always dreamt will happen.

What do you want to do in your life that feels scary, and how can you take action on this thing?

Chapter 3
Becoming a star

I'm glad to say that I never let my shyness stop me in my career, although there have been ups and downs. I might not have been loud but I had a quiet confidence. When I was in a place where I felt comfortable, I was able to shine, but when I wasn't happy, I struggled to fit in.

My first full time job was a bit of a disaster, and looking back I know that I was bullied. But I didn't know what to do about it at the time. Working in the restaurant of a small family-run hotel, it was an accepted norm in those days that chefs would shout and swear at the staff, but I wonder how that would be accepted now, over 20 years later.

It was tough being in an environment

every day where I was made to feel that I wasn't good enough. I'm sure it was nothing personal, but if any of the staff did something wrong, like taking an order incorrectly or getting in the way, then the retaliations certainly felt personal. Of course, it was a highly pressurised environment, but the managers turned the other cheek and ignored it.

Statistics indicate that half of us have quit a job because of our boss, and that's happened to me on more than this one occasion, although thankfully in less extreme situations.

As a shy girl, it's not always easy to stand up for yourself, particularly when you are working with a dominant personality. It can be easier to back down or withdraw from the situation. It was only later in my career that I realised how personality styles impact on how you think and react to situations, and how you can modify your behaviour to cope with this.

After being shouted at one too many times, I became fed up with the resulting feelings of anxiety, and the migraines that started around that time, so it wasn't long before I started job hunting. But I still stuck it out for seven months before I left and found something new. And being shy, it did take me longer to get to know people and build effective relationships. I was more likely to withdraw and appear unapproachable, especially when in a difficult situation, rather than stand up for myself.

But luckily my second full time job was a happier experience. Working for the Hilton Hotel Group, I loved my job working in reception, greeting guests and being 'front of house', although you might wonder if that should have been the mouse's worst nightmare! But here's the thing: as the mouse, the more I worked with other people and had positive experiences, the more I relaxed, stopped worrying and started talking.

Each year the Hilton Group held an awards ceremony in London where they recognised their staff for a job well done. Around ten people from each hotel were taken to the Park Lane Hilton Hotel for a glitzy and opulent gala dinner, and in 1995 I was one of those chosen by our manager to go away for the night. There were hundreds of people in the room, everyone dressed up in their finery and a lot of wine was being consumed too!

When it came to the awards announcements, I was there clapping and cheering other people, and then suddenly my name was called out as the 'Star of the Year' for the Portsmouth hotel. Stunned, I walked up to the stage to collect my award, which I still have to this day. I can't remember what I said, as I never expected to be acknowledged, but I certainly felt pride and pleasure as I stood there in the limelight.

That feeling when Paul Bean, my general manager , believed in me enough to nominate me for this award was a significant milestone. Coming from the bullying environment of my previous job to one where I felt appreciated was, with hindsight, an important moment in my life. I'm sure that my manager never realised how much of an impact this had on me and my future career – so thank you! We all need someone to believe in us and champion us, and I will never forget those who made the biggest difference.

Becoming a star

Shy girl tip – Expand your comfort zone

When you're in your comfort zone, you'll be comfortable and never grow. You'll be like 90% of the population – having a mediocre life, getting by, and being average.

I'm wondering ... What do you need to do to expand your comfort zone? What can you do to stretch it?

The more you stretch your comfort zone, the bigger it will become, and the more comfortable you'll feel doing those things that used to scare you. You just need to take steps to live life to the full, leading to fulfilment, greater confidence and the chance to have the lifestyle you desire.

Chapter 4
The light bulb moment

On a personal note, I never let my introversion prevent me from living my life and doing what I wanted to do. In 1997, as well as moving in with Peter, I flew to Canada by myself to meet up with my friend Zoe, who was taking some time out to travel. We backpacked from Vancouver to Toronto for a month, travelling by train and bus – and had a whale of a time!

On the work front, I moved every few years to a new job, developing my skills and finding out more about myself along the way. After working my way up the ranks in various international hotel chains, I briefly became an NVQ assessor before establishing a career in human resources and doing my CIPD (Chartered Institute of Personnel and Development) postgraduate qualification.

I also found out about personality profiling in 2003, which is something I knew about but had never studied before. That idea that we are all different; who'd have thought?

This was a key moment, as part of me thought I needed to change and should be more outgoing and sociable. I'm sure I'm not the only person who feels that they should conform to a certain way, thus suppressing the core part of their personality. I was lucky enough to start that journey of self-awareness and understanding myself, and this also enabled me to appreciate the personal styles of others.

Based on the Jung philosophy, the system that I studied was DISC, which measures your behaviour and personality style, which are assessed thorough completing a short questionnaire. Although it's not about putting people into boxes, the system provides an insight into your preferred behavioural style, your strengths and limitations and what motivates you. It's a questionnaire that's often used as part of a recruitment process, appraisals, career development and to develop teams.

The manufacturing company I was working for decided that it would be useful to introduce this tool to the company, and as a member of the human resources team, I was one of those who was lucky enough to be trained. It was a life changer. Not only did I complete my profile and start to know myself more, **I understood why I found it easier to get on with certain people and struggled to develop relationships with others.**

So that you're not in the dark, let me share some of the technical jargon with you.

What is DISC?

DISC is an acronym, which stands for:

D = Dominance
I = Influence
S = Steadiness
C = Compliance

Once you complete the questionnaire that takes around seven minutes, you receive a report that will help you to understand:

- Your strengths and limitations
- How you like to communicate with others
- How you cope with stress
- How you manage situations that may cause conflict
- How you make decisions
- How you are motivated and what may cause you fear

In a nutshell, everyone has a combination of one or more styles as a working strength. As with many questionnaires like this, there are no rights or wrongs

The light bulb moment

and no good or bad profiles. When you get to understand yourself, the important thing is not to change into someone else, but work out how you can be most effective.

If you are a **dominant person**, you will come across as direct, assertive and forceful. If you are strong in this area, you'll be results driven and thrive in a challenging and competitive environment. You're great in a crisis, will make quick decisions and take action. On the downside you dislike routine situations and can easily lose interest once a challenge has gone.

Influencers are great people persons. You will be positive, persuasive and like to build relationships with others. Motivated by recognition, you will be very communicative and will manage people by selling your ideas to them to get them on board. On the downside, you won't enjoy making decisions that put you in an unfavourable light, such as disciplining others, and may find it difficult to see things through to conclusion.

If you are a **steady person**, you will crave peace and security. You will come across as kind, patient and amiable, and will be a great listener. A persistent person, you will manage by organising and will communicate by listening to others. You will be great in a specialist or administrative role and will organise yourself and others well. On the downside, you don't particularly like change unless you've been involved every step of the way.

If you are **compliant**, you will be motivated by rules and procedures. You will come across as careful, systematic, logical and precise and may be seen as a perfectionist. You will want facts to support everything that you do, which may frustrate colleagues who prefer an overview of a situation, and you will come across as cautious and considered in your approach.

The light bulb moment

When I did my profile for the first time, it affirmed what I knew already. With an SCI profile – strengths in the Steadiness, Compliance and Influence areas – I liked a quiet life; I was structured, organised and sought assurance. But it also made me realise that other people weren't the same as me, and that I could adapt my behaviour accordingly. **I was able to recognise the behaviours of others and change my approach.**

Let me give you an example. One of my bosses was very direct in her style. At the time her behaviour was difficult to handle as there was a lack of softness in her approach. She wanted something and she wanted it now! Sometimes directness can come across in an aggressive way, and it can be difficult to handle if that's not your style.

What this did mean, however, is that I could be direct back. Actually she preferred me to be direct rather than pussyfooting around a subject. She didn't want waffle. She just wanted the facts of a situation and preferred me to be straight with her. I wasn't being rude or aggressive; **I was just**

presenting things to her in a way that best suited her. Also I stopped taking it so personally when she was direct with me.

You may think: Doesn't it take superhuman strength to change your approach to every person? Well, of course you don't have to do it in every single interaction. Some people you are just not going to gel with and that's life. However, as a naturally shy person, I found it brilliant to understand the personality styles of the key people I lived and worked with to see how I could get on with them better. For me, that was the light bulb moment.

The profile process also helped me to understand how I cope with stress, because when you complete your own DISC profile, one of the elements demonstrates this in black and white. As I inferred in the prologue, I've always been one of those people who is calm on the outside, but it doesn't take much for me to transform into a volcano, quick to blow and quick to simmer. This was something that was particularly dominant during my teenage years, so if I'd understood myself earlier, it would have made an incredible difference to my life.

Being a structured and methodical person, knowing my profile has helped me to play to my strengths and do those things where I excel. As you'll find out later, although I'm not one to be the centre of attention, by understanding myself better, I was able to put systems in place that allowed me to do this more easily.

It also helped me to find out what I wanted to change. I preferred to think things through in my head before articulating them out loud. It made me aware of what I could do differently and how I could change my approach.

Subsequently, I went on to study Emotional Intelligence, another great learning. Again in the form of a questionnaire, followed by completing a diploma in the topic, this also helped me to understand myself, and later also enabled me to support my clients better and teach it to groups.

How to become more self-aware

One of the things that helped me was to become more self-aware, which I'll share with you further now.

Being self-aware is about being able to understand yourself better and being aware of your...

- Goals – short and long term (what you want to achieve and how you will do this)
- Beliefs – about yourself and others (both positive and negative, your fears and anxieties, confidence and self-belief)
- Values – those things you hold dear (both personal and work values)
- Drivers – that affect how you work (and your hot buttons that might make you react in a certain way)
- Rules – that you live by: the shoulds, musts and oughts
- Self-talk – that tells you whether you can or

The light bulb moment

cannot do something

... and the ways in which these impact on what you do.

Each of these manifests itself in your internal and external behaviour and how you display your emotions and respond to other people's emotions. One way of becoming more self-aware is to pay attention to what you actually see and hear and not what you think you see and hear. Your beliefs, values, drivers and rules act as filters: distorting, deleting or generalising what otherwise might be important information.

All too often these filters get in the way of how you use this information when it hits your senses. This means that the things that you believe are true will impact on how you interpret a situation or react when something is said to you. Think about what happens when someone gives you feedback; your reaction will probably be different dependent on how you've been praised or criticised in the past, and whether it triggers a particular memory or experience.

The higher your level of self-awareness, the greater your ability to recognise and distinguish between what is fact and what is actually the result of applying one of your filters.

You may, however, not be aware of this initially as much of what we do is driven by our subconscious. Imagine an iceberg, where you can only see the top 10–20%, which is the stuff that is conscious – your skills and knowledge. Below the surface are your values, beliefs, motives and traits, which drive you and influence what you do. The more you know yourself, the easier it will be to change the things that no longer serve you.

To be emotionally intelligent, you need to understand yourself (including the things under the surface):

- Your personal style
- Your strengths and weaknesses
- How your feelings affect you
- Your openness to feedback and development
- Your self-confidence based on your strengths
- Your impact on others
- Your non-verbal behaviour
- Your energy levels

You are unique with both internal and external dimensions to your personality. It is important to understand your own personal style and how this can impact on others and affect your judgements and the decisions you make.

Shy girl tip – Understand what makes you tick

We are all different and you don't have to do your DISC personal profile to recognise the nuances in every personality. But I hope that reading this will help you to understand how you work, what makes you tick and how you prefer to behave in different situations.

Given the descriptions I shared with you earlier, where do you think your strengths lie? If you have difficult relationships where communication is key, what might be contributing towards these difficulties?

As the late Stephen Covey said, "seek to understand and then to be understood", and success in relationship building comes down to being able to temporarily adapt your behaviour style when you are communicating with others. When you can understand what makes other people tick, it makes it easier to do things differently when you need to.

The light bulb moment

The mouse that roars

Chapter 5
Becoming a life coach

In October 2005, Peter and I finally got married, a quiet affair in a beautiful hotel, as neither of us enjoys the limelight. But like many things that intense, it had been all-consuming since getting engaged in Reykjavík on my thirtieth birthday, and then organising the wedding. It wasn't until we returned from our honeymoon that I realised that something had to change at work.

January 2006 was a pivotal time in my life. Working in a male-dominated environment at the time, my role in human resources involved a lot of analysis and detail, something you'd imagine that I'd be suited to, but I was pretty bored.

The kiss of death and big tipping point was the moment that my boss said to me **"Karen, I wish you'd speak out more"**. This was the catalyst to make a change. At the time the words hindered me, but in hindsight, it was one of the best things that could have happened. I've never been one to make a quick decision without research first, but at that juncture in my career, I needed to do something new; I just wasn't sure what. I didn't want to go back into something that I wouldn't enjoy, and I knew that the grass wasn't always greener on the other side. The constant searching in my life for something different made me realise that I didn't have to accept the status quo, so with a sense of trepidation I took myself online to find someone to help me.

I'd heard of this thing called life coaching. I had plenty of books on this and other self-development topics, and started to explore it further. I was unhappy with my work life, so it seemed like the perfect antidote. When I searched on the internet for this term, I was overwhelmed with choice. When you are choosing someone to work with on an intimate and personal basis, it can be hard to know where to start, but I decided to take a leap of faith. And I found my first life coach on ebay in January 2006.

Yes, you read that right! I found my first coach on ebay: a lady who was advertising her services to the highest bidder, which turned out to be me. When I found out I'd won, my heart was pounding as I didn't know what was going to happen next. I'd stepped up to the plate to make a new change in my life, and change isn't easy when you're reticent and reserved. But I also knew that I couldn't continue where I was; I had to do something new, and I went on to employ this coach for the next few months.

I realised that if I was unhappy, I could do something about it. The first thing we worked on was my career. I started to really understand my strengths, which wasn't an easy thing for someone like me as I've never been one to shout about my talents, although knowing where I struggled was a given! Working out what I was actually good at and where I excelled took a while. However, it wasn't long before I had two interviews, and a job offer for the role of human resources advisor at my local college. I could see how my new manager would allow me to play to my strengths as a trainer, and I'd be in an environment where I could thrive. So I handed in my notice and started to get ready for the change.

Yet that wasn't the best thing about this experience; I also realised that I had found a vocation that I wanted to pursue. I decided to become a coach. What I didn't realise at the time was that I was about to start a journey to become the mouse that roars.

Looking back, I jumped into my coaching

training very quickly. After attending a two day free introductory coaching weekend in Brighton, the company's effective sales technique meant that I'd signed up for the full Personal Coaching Diploma by the following Friday!

This was the first major monetary investment of my life. Up until this point, any significant training and development had been paid for by the organisation that I'd worked for, and I also wasn't sure what I was going to do with my qualification. I thought I'd probably work for myself, but having been a corporate employee up to this point, I didn't have a clue where to start.

The training got me focused, and one of the traits of being an SCI personality means that I am a completer-finisher, so I didn't hang around with my training. Although the big conference rooms full of people didn't fulfil my favoured learning style, working through the modules by myself was something I found easier. I wasn't fazed by the huge folders of information and methodically worked through the steps.

The great thing about any personal development is that you work on your own stuff too. You can't learn to be a coach without experiencing it yourself and taking part in the activities. Our training weekends gave me the chance to work with others, to experience coaching myself and to try things out in a safe environment. They also gave me the chance to meet and experience new teachers who inspired me, and meet new people, some of whom went on to become good friends, even if I felt out of my depth at times. One of the things about being a shy person is that sometimes shyness comes across as being aloof, and it can take me a while to get to know and trust people. But when I do, the friendships are long-lasting.

At that moment in my life, I learnt what was important to me. Of course, this took me out of my comfort zone, yet I lapped up the learning, engaging my brain cells. It was something that made so much sense and something that I knew would help others.

Like many coaches, one of the reasons for doing it was to make a difference. Since experiencing it myself initially, I knew the impact it could make, and I wanted to support people who, like me, had been struggling. But even though I qualified as a coach in November 2006, I didn't quite get what it would mean to run a coaching business.

Within coaching, there are various tools and techniques

that you can use on yourself and with your clients. One of these is the wheel of life which helps you to work out where you are now, where you want to be, and the gap between the two places, which is one of the fundamentals of coaching. There's also the values and beliefs work which looks at what's important to you, so that you can get more of what's vital to you in your life. When everything feels aligned, and you can get over things that sabotage you, life is easier.

We learn about life through our relationships with our parents, our peers and our teachers, without questioning the impact of these thoughts. That's why the training was so powerful as it enabled me to understand what was important. I recognised the impact of my childhood on me as an adult and how these experiences affected my choices and my values. I now know that I crave security and safety, that integrity and honesty are important to me, as well as love and connection, learning and personal growth.

I also worked out that one of the reasons that I needed to leave that job in 2006 was that my values no longer matched those of my employer, which I find happens to many people – I just didn't realise this at the time. There was a mismatch with my aspirations, what was important to me, and I couldn't see how my role would grow into something that would fulfil me.

Discovering coaching opened up a whole new world for me – of characters, experiences and concepts that I'd never heard of before. I came across Tony Robbins, who I'll talk about further later, who said that "Values are like a compass that directs your life". Just understanding this will help you to become more in control of your actions and emotions, make better decisions as you know what is important, recognise what you need to do to feel good, and find different ways to fulfil your values rather than continuing down the same old path as before.

Personally I started to recognise where I respected my values and where I didn't, and what I needed to do to make sure these were reflected in my life. I found out what I wanted more of (my 'towards' values) – I enjoyed alone time, I preferred the intimacy of one-to-one connections, and liked the reassuring nature of home comforts. I also realised what I wanted less of (my 'away from' values) – being in busy and noisy places, discourtesy and lack of respect, and being challenged on those things that are important to me.

I also learnt about what stopped me, and

where I sabotaged my successes and failed to grow, although it took a while for this to really sink in!

Shy girl tip – Understand what you're good at

One of the things that many people struggle with is realising what they are actually good at, and if you're struggling in this area, then let me help you out.

There are a couple of things you can do:

Write down 5 things that you think you're good at. Don't edit or question yourself as you go as this isn't going to help you to get 5 things down on paper. If you're struggling with this, think about your qualifications, experiences, skills, and capabilities.

Once you've got this list, for each of the items, write down why you're good at this thing. This will help to reinforce your responses and get into the detail of how you excel in this area.

Ask your friends, colleagues or clients what they think you're good at, as you often can't see what other people see and this will enhance your view of yourself.

The mouse that roars

Chapter 6
Anything is possible

Audrey Hepburn said, "Nothing is impossible; the word itself says 'I'm possible'!" As a trainee coach, I believed that.

But in reality, so many people fail to sit down and consider what they'd love to do. It's easier to stay on the treadmill of life wondering how or if you'll ever get off. Most people stick to that area of comfort where they do the same thing day in day out and never make the changes that they want to make. They ignore the pain and carry on regardless. The ifs, buts and maybes get in the way of what they'd love to do.

That's one of the reasons I trained to be a coach; I saw the light at the end of the tunnel and knew that one could reach it, even if it seemed like a tiny speck in the distance at the starting point.

I realised that I had found my vocation and what I wanted to do. But if it was that easy,

The mouse that roars

this would be a very short book! When I qualified as a coach in November 2006, I set up my business, Self Discovery Coaching. I had no qualms about creating a website myself, and getting some business cards printed, as these seemed like the most important things to do at the time. But guess what? Getting my business off the ground didn't happen as easily as I'd imagined.

You have to remember that I'd always been this naturally shy girl; and in my naivety, I expected the business to come to me, without having to stretch and do new things, and move out of my comfort zone. I had bought in to the hype that was built up during our training – that we could attract high-paying clients and have a profitable business – yet we were not taught what we needed to do to actually get there. I had been in a corporate environment for all of my working life, and I did not have a clue where to start with running a business!

Thinking back to those days, I can imagine myself standing on the doorstep of my house, holding my coaching certificate in both hands, shaking it around, waving it above my head, tentatively whispering "I'm here". And guess what, nobody heard me!

It's no good finding your vocation if you aren't ready to step up, and certainly in the early days of running a business, no one knows that you exist (unless you tell them). Plus I made some mistakes when I started. I sold coaching! Who buys coaching? In the UK, it is a concept that wasn't as prominent in 2006 as it is now. Although it was a growing industry, people certainly didn't buy into coaching, but they would buy into the outcome, result or solution that solved their pain, problem or difficulty. I didn't understand this until much later.

I was told I needed to niche, so initially I vaguely niched as a coach helping women with work-life balance. How successful do you think I was? Appealing to 50% of the population with a wishy-washy message just wasn't going to work!

Although I knew what I loved to do in terms of coaching, I didn't know how I could turn this love into a business. I knew (deep down) that remaining that mouse was no longer an option. I also realised that having a passion to make a difference was going to help me to overcome the fear that held me back. I had to start somewhere, so I did.

The mouse that roars

Whenever you make any type of change in life, you just have to go for it. Even if you look back later and wonder what on earth you were thinking about!

Shy girl tip – The worry buster technique

When you find yourself becoming anxious or are worried about undertaking a task that you've never done before, like a presentation, setting up a business, or something else, try out the worry buster technique.

Go through the following questions in your mind or write down the answers on a piece of paper. What I love about this exercise is that if you're doing it with someone else, it can be done content free, i.e. you don't need to know what the other person is worrying about.

Where is the evidence for the way you are thinking?

What is the logic in your interpretation?

What do you have to lose if you do/say this?

Anything is possible

What do you have to gain if you do/say this?

What would be the worst thing that could happen if you do/don't do this?

What can you learn from doing/not doing this?

What specific steps can you take to improve upon the worst possible outcome or create the best possible outcome?

The mouse that roars

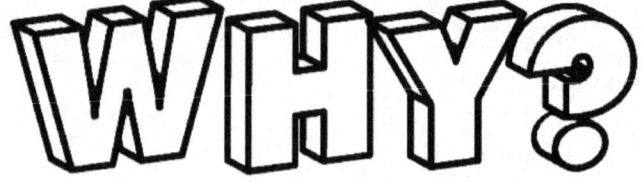

Chapter 7
Getting in touch with my why

The entrepreneur Simon Sinek says, "People don't buy what you do; they buy why you do it", a concept I discovered later, but an important one to mention here. Getting in touch with **why** you are doing something is certainly something that has spurred me on in my business, even during the most difficult of moments.

'Why' is a funny old word – one that we are encouraged not to use when we train as coaches, one that is analytical, potentially threatening or accusatory, but when used in the right way, gets meaningful results. Why is a powerful word, one that allows you to explore your dreams, your reality and the difference between the two. It's a word that can build you, empower you and help you to do something very different.

When you are doing something you love but you're not getting results – like I was in the first six months of my business –

remembering why you are doing something is incredibly important. Otherwise it is very easy to give up and go back to the thing that you wanted to move away from in the first place!

Your why is simply the reason why you are doing something. It is your driver, the passion that fuels your purpose; it's the thing that gets you up in the morning to take on a new task, and the reason behind what you do.

It's more than having a goal or objective; it's about a feeling, emotion or pull you get towards achieving your bigger vision. When this big why is fired up and set alight, amazing things can take place.

When I became a coach, I wanted to change the world, but soon realised that I could only do it one day and one person at a time, and my perseverance towards achieving that end goal certainly kept me focused. It was later on in my business that I found a way of doing this better by encouraging and inspiring other people to write their books, as well as writing my own, thus changing more lives and making a bigger difference.

Getting in touch with my why

Actually it was my why that has put this book in front of you right now, as if I hadn't had this passion in the first place, I wouldn't still be here, I wouldn't have stepped up to write this, my fourth book, and I would have stayed in a job rather than ventured out on my own. Wouldn't that have been safer for someone like me?

However, when you know why you're doing something, it makes achieving it so much easier. It goes deeper than having a passion or an urge. It's a question I'll always ask my clients, whether they are growing their business, writing their book or doing anything else to improve their life.

I employed my first business coach, Allison Marlowe, during the early days of running my business, because I knew I had a lot to learn. I met her during the free introductory coaching weekend, and I'm now pleased to call her a good friend. I remember her telling me that once you know why you're doing something, the how will come! This is a mantra that I've shared with my clients ever since.

It's also always been important for me to not do everything myself. You can't be a specialist in every single area of business. Since the early days I've had support to learn the strategies and shortcuts to running a business by having a Virtual

Assistant (VA) and support team to help me with the things that I didn't know. However, having a naturally inquisitive mind, I like to try things out and find out how things work. That's led to having a good technical knowledge and being comfortable in learning digital marketing techniques as well as offline strategies to grow my business.

As I mentioned earlier, when you understand yourself it makes it easier to see what drives you. That's why I hope you'll find the following tip useful. A few of these styles certainly resonate with me, although I'll leave you to guess which they are!

Shy girl tip – Know your drivers

One of the things that has helped me in my business is to understand what drives me, as there are many reasons why people behave differently from each other.

One concept of transactional analysis (developed by Dr Eric Berne in the 1950s) is that everyone has drivers, which are established early in childhood. They stem from the environment around you and the way you are treated by other people. Messages that were given to you when you were young can influence how you go on to think and behave as an adult.

Drivers are characteristic ways of behaving, which are usually strengths, but may become weaknesses under stress.

There are five identified drivers. You may find that you identify with a couple and you may recognise some in other people.

Be Perfect

If your style is Be Perfect, it means that you will be really good at doing accurate detailed reports, you will be neat in your appearance and you will value cleanliness and tidiness. However, it can also mean that you believe that everything you do has to be absolutely right. You may not be satisfied with anything that you do because, in your eyes, it will never be good enough. Delegation may be difficult because it is hard to trust others to do it right or other people may find it difficult to accept your standards.

Hurry Up

If Hurry Up is your preferred style, you will get a great deal done in a short period of time; however, you may find yourself overloaded and take on too much. You will always be in a hurry, often late for meetings, and always leaving things until the last moment before you do them. You may find that you end up with too many appointments in one day and may appear impatient to others.

Try Hard

If you have the Try Hard style, you will love new projects and new things to do, and work well under pressure. You are likely to have the belief that your personal value comes from the amount of effort you put into things. It is possible that you become more committed to trying rather than succeeding. Others can become frustrated that you turn small jobs into large ones to increase the amount of effort you can put in.

Be Strong

If you have the Be Strong style, you are great in a crisis, but can come across as aloof. You believe that your own value comes from not revealing your feelings, by being the one who takes everything on your own shoulders rather than asking for help. In turn, other people can assume you are unemotional and don't need positive strokes.

Please Others

If you have the Please Others style, you will be a great team member, and like to please other people. You will believe that you must always do what others ask of you in order to be valuable. You feel guilty about saying no, even when the request is unreasonable. You may find that you accept work or invitations from others instead of working on your own priorities. In turn, other people can become frustrated by your attempts to please them and interpret your actions as being insincere.

Manage your drivers

I hope these descriptions have helped you to identify what drives you. It is useful to recognise these in yourself and others, as it helps you to work to your strengths.

Self-awareness helps you to identify how you can change the way you think and behave to be more effective. So, you could choose to change your behaviours in one of the following ways.

If your style is Be Perfect, believe that you're good enough as you are.

If Hurry Up is your thing, take your time.

If you Try too Hard, just do it for a change!

If you feel that you need to Be Strong, take the opportunity to be open and express your needs from time to time.

If you need to Please Others, please yourself for a change!

Chapter 8
Just feel the fear and...

I make no bones about the fact that I struggled during the early stages of running my business, but it's also important to acknowledge that I didn't give up. When I was in that place, I put out my feelers to get some pro bono clients to give me a chance to practise and hone my skills. One of these people later went on to pay me and I started to get a trickle of people who were interested in what I did. I'll never forget the joy of getting my first paying client. I even photocopied the cheque and would have framed it and put it on my wall if I'd been bold enough to do so!

I must admit that during the early days I wasn't so sure of myself. When I had a call with a client, I was inclined to lay out all of my coaching notes in front of me (just in case I forgot the questions I *should* be asking!), but it didn't take long before I trusted myself and my intuition rather than just what I was taught. As I tell many of my clients now, once you've done your training, you'll develop your own style, find out what works for you, and do it your way.

One of my first lucky breaks was when I was contacted by a large multinational pharmaceutical company after they found me through my website – so I knew I was doing something right! I was still employed at that stage, and I remember sneaking out of my office and taking the call on the stairs along the corridor. I was asked to put in a proposal for some coaching and training work using DISC profiling with their senior sales team. I put in my first ever proposal and quoted for the work. A few weeks later, they accepted it and we agreed the first training date.

The training took place in a village nestled in the Derbyshire countryside, and I remember taking a couple of days off work to deliver it and travelling to stay at a hotel nearby. My husband came with me and stayed at the hotel for a bit of moral support. As the shy girl, you can imagine how I felt. But the great thing about DISC is that I know my stuff, and I also knew the profiles of the people I was meeting before I arrived. This helped me to understand what to expect, and the type of people I was working with. One of the advantages of my profile is that I'm a steady, process-driven person who likes people, and when I am 100% confident in what I'm teaching, I easily get into flow. It's being put on the spot that I don't like! I was still nervous, but I was paid well for a day's work. And I obviously did a good job as they commissioned me to roll out the training with the whole team, which I did over the coming 12 months.

It was this opportunity that kept me in business, as it gave me the confidence to make it happen and to believe that I could do it. During that period, there was only one member of staff who didn't get the point of the training, but due to his profile I was already aware of the potential difficulties I might face working with him! Of course, you could call that a self-fulfilling prophecy, but it also helped me to turn him around by the end of the day's training.

My strategy was to feel the fear and do it anyway. I could easily have ignored my first corporate opportunity. I could have shied away from getting clients and I could have sabotaged my success. I also learnt that I wasn't perfect; I knew that when I felt uncomfortable I had a tendency to blush, that I sometimes stumbled over my words, and I

Just feel the fear and...

didn't always get things right. But unless you try, how will you know?

Another of these experiences when I felt the fear was networking, which was one of those things that I knew that I should do in business! I remember one of my first experiences of networking, which was a total disaster.

The event itself was in a town I wasn't familiar with, so when I arrived, I parked on the road and eventually found the venue for the event. As I located the other members of the group, I realised that they were a collection of smartly dressed men, who seemed serious about business. Then there was me, feeling like a fraud and uncertain, with a message that was unclear, feeling out of my depth and very much an amateur. This didn't bode well. And that wasn't the worst thing... As I left the networking group late at night, I forgot where I'd parked my car!

Of course I had a choice after that situation. I could have given up at that point because I felt small, insignificant and I didn't really feel that I had a 'proper' business like the men around me. But I didn't.

I started to find the networking groups that worked for

me and began to build a group of supportive people around me who were also in business. They 'got' who I was and where I was coming from. Some became my clients and some I employed to help me, and others have remained brilliant friends and contacts to this day.

Defining my message helped as well. In a way that very first networking event was a blessing, as I realised that I needed to get clearer on my area of expertise. So I worked on what I wanted to stand for and who I wanted to help. Once I got that, it was easier to grow my business. With my experience in human resources, interviewing dozens of people, and having seen hundreds if not thousands of CVs, at the time I felt my expertise lay in helping people with their careers, and I focused on helping women who wanted to find a career that they loved.

From a technical point of view, I was pretty clued up about what to do initially. I had my website and started to create a list of people interested in what I did, even though the first 30 people consisted of my mum and dad, friends and family! It started to grow and I created my first 'Career health check' report to generate leads on my website. I later began to blog, and wrote a regular newsletter. If I look back now at the website copy, I know that it vastly improved over time, but it still got me business and helped me to attract clients.

Everything I did helped me to move forward towards my ultimate aim of running a successful business. I just did it the mouse way. There were things that I found daunting, like having a sales conversation with a client and feeling confident with my packages. To counteract this, I carried out pretend practice sessions with a fellow coach to stop my voice rising to a high squeaky pitch when I quoted my fees!

I made myself do speaking engagements. Although I'm a qualified trainer and have had plenty of experience speaking in front of groups, the thought of doing it as part of my own business was scary. There's also a difference between training people and being an influential speaker. At one of my first talks I remember feeling hotter and hotter, redder and redder as I grabbed hold of my notes and kept a firm view of my PowerPoint slides. However now I'm more likely to go with the flow rather than have a set agenda, and find out what the audience want to hear from me and deliver this to them.

Importantly, I made a difference with my clients. I managed to find those who needed my help and, through the contacts I'd made, it was easier to grow my business and get noticed by the people who needed me.

In those days, most of my clients were individuals who had heard me speak, found me via my website or newsletter, or had been referred to me by a mutual contact. I worked with a range of individuals, many of whom were facing career change (just like I had), wanting to increase their confidence and get support to take the next steps at work. I also did some corporate work that came along, delivering training on a diverse number of topics in organisations across the UK.

I believe that much of my success during these early years in business was due to the fact that I was willing to step out of my rut, my mediocre life, where things were average and could sometimes be fearful, into an area where I was going to be more fulfilled, fearless, and courageous and have the confidence to do things that scared me. Also, when you stretch your comfort zone, what happens? The things that once scared you aren't so frightening any more as you develop and grow as a person, which is what happened to me.

If you feel fear, don't let those fears stop you from doing something. Rationally think about the pros and cons and what you'll gain from making it happen. There are many times in our lives when we have to take a risk and can't be sure of the outcome, but if you didn't do it, how would you feel?

I believe in taking action, and I also believe in serendipity. Sometimes it's in those moments of despair that the right things fall into your lap or you bump into someone who you haven't seen for ages and they have the perfect opportunity for you.

Just a simple thing like smiling at someone and saying hi over a cup of tea at a networking event can lead to a beautiful friendship and this is one of the reasons why you're reading this book today. It's because of one particular lady whom I met at a networking event, Esther Harris, that this book is in your hands, as she is the lady who helped me to create it!

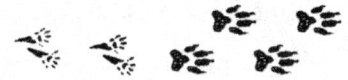

Shy girl tip – Creating virtuous circles

Your beliefs have a critical effect on your state or experiences. If you believe that you can't do something, that you are not worthy, or that you are not good enough, what do you think is going to happen? On the converse side, what do you think will happen if you do believe you can do something, you are worthy and you are good enough?

Here's something to remember:

Your beliefs affect your thoughts
Your thoughts affect your actions
Your actions affect your results
And your results affect your beliefs.

Think of this as a circle, linking through the four stages. You have a choice about whether to create vicious circles or virtuous circles.

Just feel the fear and...

If you always believe that you are good enough, you are going to get a different outcome to one where you are convinced that you will fail/can't do something/are fearful (or insert any other belief you have into this sentence!).

Let me leave you with this famous quote.

> "If you always think what you have always thought,
> Then you will always feel what you have always felt;
> If you always feel what you have always felt,
> Then you will always do what you have always done;
> If you always do what you have always done,
> Then you will always get what you have always gotten;
> If you always get what you have always gotten,
> Then you will always think what you have always thought." – Socrates

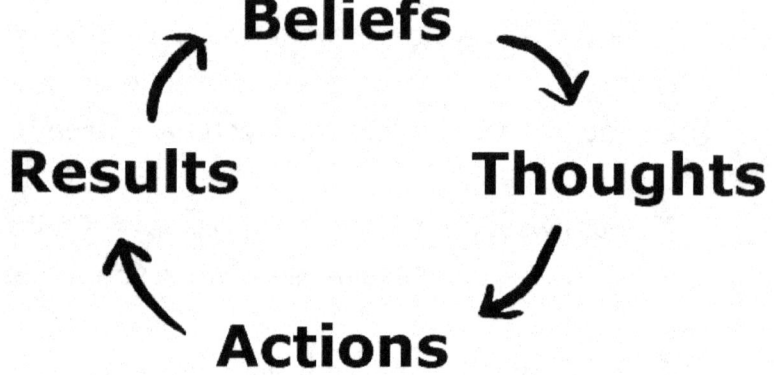

Chapter 9
Taking one step at a time

In many ways I believe that things happen for a reason, and in February 2008, I walked on burning hot coals for the first time in my life. My mentor had a spare ticket for Tony Robbins' Unleash the Power Within event, and connected me with two other ladies attending, Wendy Wyatt and Roberta Jerram.

The first time we met was at Wendy's house at 6am on the day we were to travel to London. I never realised, at this point, how pivotal these ladies were going to be in the next stage of my business and in my life. During this weekend, we got to know each other extremely well – probably even more so as we drove up together, shared a triple room and didn't sleep much! That instant connection resulted in sharing things that we'd rarely talked about before.

I have to say that going to one of Tony

The mouse that roars

Robbins' events isn't for the faint-hearted! After we queued up for hours with thousands of other people to register, I wasn't prepared for the loud music, high energy, American feel of that convention room! As we walked tentatively into the room, the noise bounced off the walls and the vibe was catching.

Although I don't like being in places with lots of other people (many thousands in this situation), I'll never regret that weekend. Apart from coaching and a two day diploma in NLP (Neuro Linguistic Programming), I'd never worked on myself so intensively. He took me deep into some of the programming, beliefs and stories that I'd been telling myself and helped me to change the way I thought. It was pretty intensive work and Tony doesn't stop going – the days started early and finished very late!

The most important message that I got from this weekend was the power of the mind. Like many people, I often had thoughts like "I'm not good enough", "I'm not ready to do that yet", or "I'll start that when...". And I also found it easy to sabotage my success by listening to others and forgetting to listen to my heart and my true calling.

One of the things that Tony said, which has always stayed with me, is that we have 65,000 thoughts every day and 95% of these were the same as yesterday. This means that 95% of them are likely to be the same as tomorrow, so doesn't it make sense that these thoughts are empowering, motivating and positive?

Our thoughts affect our mindset and if you are more positive, you will feel more resourceful and happier, and the words you use to tell yourself things will impact on how you feel. You have a choice about what that self-talk says to you and the language it uses. Ultimately how you run your brain affects how you run your life. These learnings are reflected in some of the habits I have in place now like gratitude, journaling and meditation.

By the way, I'm certainly not perfect, but I've just learnt to have a more positive outlook, even when things go wrong – and they do – and I'm sure that this will be the same for you. But you have a choice about how to deal with situations. You can dwell on the negatives, wallow in self-pity or tell everyone your sob story, and this is fine as it can help you to cope with the situation. But if you want to have a better life, then learn how to frame or reframe what has taken place.

You can view disappointments as learning opportunities, you can look back at disasters as a chance to find out what not to do, and you can view problems as opportunities (sorry, I know it's a cliché!).

Changing the meaning of a situation or the cause and effect of what has happened will affect you and your life and the way you view new experiences in the future too.

This internal voice was particularly important during the weekend when I experienced my first firewalk. It certainly takes mind over matter, especially when there are thousands of people joining you! Like life, it is about taking one step at a time, slowly but surely, focusing on how you're going to achieve your goals.

As we walked barefoot towards the dozens of steaming firewalks, the parallel stretches of burning coals, chanting "Yes, yes, yes!", I felt certain that I could do this, and I said "Cool moss, cool moss" as I walked over the burning hot coals, which was fine until I looked down and thought "Hot coals" and left with a small burn on the back of my heel! But I still felt a great deal of satisfaction and joy as I walked across the cold tarmac back into the conference hall.

You don't have to walk on hot coals to experience certainty and remove your fears, but if you do, it will be one of the best experiences you've ever had! There's something about using the memory as a positive anchor that you can reinforce in the future and when you face other difficulties. Just remembering this ingrained experience will help you to dig deep.

Every success you have is a result of baby steps and sometimes big leaps. As long as every step you take is moving you in the right direction, does it really matter which you choose as long as you take strides forward every day? Of course, there will be times when it feels as though you are taking one step forward, and two steps back, but at least you are moving!

The ladies and I made a pact after the event that we'd meet up regularly to keep each other motivated. Even now, many years after the event, we have lunch or dinner together every six to eight weeks and keep the energy burning! Our lunches last way into the evening, and we've been known to go out to dinner and be standing outside for hours in the car park in the freezing cold after the pub has shut, as we still have so much to say to each other!

There's something about being inspired and invigorated; we are there to champion each other, whereas so often people are keen to criticise and pass judgement without knowing the whole situation.

Shy girl tip – Change your state, increase your energy

When we went to Tony Robbins' event we learnt to create our power move, which is the thing that you can do when you want to pump yourself up! Here's the science behind this. If you want to change your state or mood, there are three things you can change – your physiology, your focus and your terminology. As physiology will change your state by 75%, a power move is a great way to increase your energy.

Firstly you need to create your power move. This is something that you can repeat easily, like jumping on the spot, punching the air or clapping your hands. Then you can combine this movement with a simple positive phrase or word (like "yes") with upbeat music to get you motivated. Then use your power move when you need to raise your energy.

But if this feels too much, there's also a more British way to change the way you feel about something, especially if you're feeling frustrated, unsure of yourself or want to increase your energy.

Stand up now and change your posture; look down, hunch and round your shoulders and hang your head down towards the floor. How do you feel when you're like that?

Now stand up, straighten your shoulders, take a deep breath, lift your head up and smile. You will feel much more positive just by changing your posture.

You can take this further by raising your arms above your shoulders in what Amy Cuddy, in her TED Talk, calls the 'Power Pose'. How do you feel now?

The mouse that roars

Chapter 10
Modelling excellence

Following the Tony Robbins weekend, I continued to pursue my NLP training. I did the NLP Practitioner qualification in 2008 and went on to do the NLP Master Practitioner qualification in 2009. As with the Tony Robbins weekend, I spent much of that time continuing to work on my 'stuff', because to be able to use the tools and techniques with your clients, you need to be able to practise them too. I experienced moments that had a huge impact on the mouse and the story I share.

I was learning strategies that enabled me to change habits, set and achieve exciting goals, understand and change my language patterns, increase my confidence, get to grips with my values, understand and change my beliefs, and so much more. Hey, I'm just the same as everyone else; I have my foibles and shortcomings and I can sabotage myself, but I've also learnt how to manage and change these too.

One of the ways that you can change and be your best you is by spending time with other people who have done what you want to achieve, and have the mindset to push themselves further. That's why many of the best athletes and sportspeople have coaches.

This is also the reason why I chose to spend time with successful coaches and model the mindset behind a successful coaching business, when I did my modelling project as part of my NLP Master Practitioner qualification.

Modelling essentially looks at the 'ability' of an individual with respect to a particular skill for the purpose of instilling similar behavioural patterns in oneself and others. And whilst most of my group chose something small and attainable, I took a huge topic as my project. Hey, what's new!

The reason I chose this topic is because I had experienced it myself, and this became my brief:

In the first six months (or longer) after qualifying as a coach, new coaches often struggle to stay afloat.

If they are not already self-employed in a related discipline, they find this period demoralising as although they are trained to coach people, they are often given little more than cursory information about how to set up, market and grow a business. It is during this period that these new coaches sink or swim. Some are able to pursue their business successfully and others give up.

I wanted to know what the difference was **that made the difference** in terms of being successful, and why some people make it and some do not.

As well as initially finding and interviewing at least four exemplary 'models', I wanted to explore the criteria that led to their success. Within NLP you can do this through a series of questions and observation. This enabled me to identify the criteria that led to their success, what motivated them and what internal and external processes and behavioural patterns they used which enabled them to be an excellent coach and business owner.

I was looking for people who had mastered coaching, were running a successful business that met their values, goals and beliefs, who had reached the pinnacle of their career and were achieving recognition on a consistent basis, who had written a book, spoken on stage and were recognised in their field.

I was familiar with the importance of mindset, and wanted to find out what else was going on when it came to running a successful business. By the way, I defined business success (in this situation) as 'having the knowledge of how businesses really work and not just the technical knowledge about a product or service' and mindset as 'the thought processes characteristic of an individual or group; what makes someone tick'.

When I embarked on this project, I made a list of everyone whom I'd love to interview: coaches who were my role models, and people whose books were on my bookshelf. Many curious colleagues enquired later how I persuaded many of these people to be interviewed and spend time with me, and the simple answer is that I just asked for their help. Where I didn't have direct contacts, I asked people I knew (in my network) who were connected with these people to help me.

For the initial project, I interviewed the following people: Suzy Greaves (author and now editor of Psychologies magazine), Allison Marlowe (my own mentor at the time), my good friend Suparna Dhar

Modelling excellence

(now an author), Hannah McNamara (an author and exemplar for me), and Gladeana McMahon (a prolific author and chair of the Association for Coaching).

Every interview was different. I remember spending hours talking with Gladeana in her therapy room just outside London, drinking coffee and lapping up the stories. With Hannah, there was a more businesslike feel to our meeting, but I learnt extremely valuable tips from an author whose first book was well-thumbed! Allison and I met in a hotel lobby in Portsmouth, and we were oblivious to the sounds that were going on around us (which I only realised later when I played back the recording).

I drove to a National Trust café in Sussex to meet Suzy, just after she'd published her second book, and her infectious energy surrounded me. And my chat with Suparna, in my tiny hotel room in London just before an NLP training session, captured the essence of her journey and the changes we'd been on together. She'd gone from being my pretend sales call client to a flourishing coach in her own right since we'd met during our training in 2006.

What I learnt from these extraordinary people was life and business changing. Many of the things they shared with me were of a similar vein, and I knew there were many coaches who didn't know some of these basics. That's why I decided to go on to interview six more amazing and inspiring coaches and write a book about it. This book was later named *The Secrets of Successful Coaches* and some of the strategies from this book have been included in the following chapters.

These other interviewees were 'Supercoach' Michael Neill, Blaire Palmer, Dawn Breslin, Steve Marriott, Marian Way, and Duncan Brodie. The interviews took place from July to December 2009, and it was a brilliant experience to question some of the people whom I admired greatly. It makes sense that if you want to do something really well, you find someone who has already done it and spend time with them. This enables you to learn their strategies, and model the strategies that work.

Although a couple of interviews were on the phone (I realised that travelling to California to interview Michael may have been a little extreme!), I landed up travelling across the UK to spend time with these lovely people. One particular trip I remember well was a flight from Southampton to Edinburgh to interview Dawn Breslin. It was a foul day, pouring down with rain and windy, and the plane departure time meant an early start. Arriving in Edinburgh I had an hour to kill in the city centre before taking a taxi to Dawn's beautiful home, where her back garden was battling against the elements of the rough North Sea.

With the relaxing sounds of Bliss playing in the background and candle flames gently swaying in the wind, Dawn shared some of her nuggets with me. She compassionately nurtured me; one of the reasons I remember it well is because I was still raw from the death of a friend the month before, and Dawn's gentle style helped me to pull through.

Much of what I learnt has influenced me today. It was Blaire who made me realise that I didn't have to be superhuman, and Duncan who shared practical steps for marketing which I still share with my clients today. I later joined Marian to study clean language coaching, and Steve invited me to join him for an inspirational presentations skills training course. Of course, there was also Michael Neill who is still one of my idols in the coaching world, and someone who always inspires me.

The thing that still surprises me is that many of these people charge thousands and more for their services (at the time of interviewing him, Michael Neill charged

$50,000 per year to work with him!). Yet they all offered their time for free, although of course, this didn't come easy either. Here's me, a relatively new coach, not getting consistent clients, wondering if I'm good enough, and spending time with people whom I perceived to be the 'masters'. I needn't have worried though, as I was quickly put at ease, and it was certainly worth the initial angst! The thing about coaches is that many of them come into the industry because of a passion to make a difference, and many of the best coaches are generous with their time and information, and this helped me to write my first book.

Shy girl tip – Shifting your mindset

Your mindset is the number one thing that can stop you from reaching your goals, and is also the thing that can help you to live a better life. Only you can choose how you face the next challenge and whether you embrace new opportunities.

There are times when it helps you to work out where you are in terms of your mindset in relation to the problems or opportunities that you face.

Modelling excellence

Using a scale of 1–10, where is your mindset now?

If you are a 1 you are probably in a place of struggle. You may see every difficulty as a problem and you don't know where to turn to make it better. You may find yourself using the words should, ought, must but you can't find a way to see positives in any situations.

If you are in the middle, you probably feel paralysed occasionally and at other times you feel that life is in control. You may know that you are a little bit in a rut, but you are also taking action to get out of it.

You will be a 10 if you know that you are totally responsible for all of your experiences in life, you see problems as opportunities, and you feel that you are a naturally positive and optimistic person.

The mouse that roars

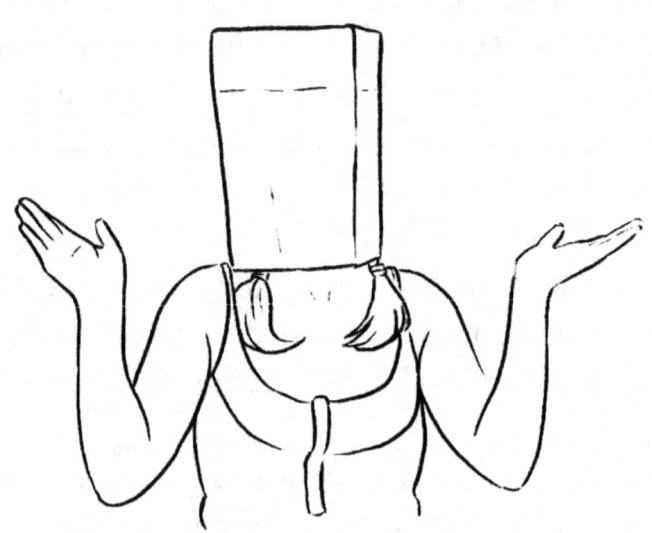

Chapter 11
The difference that makes the difference

The purpose of the modelling project was to understand the difference that made the difference when it came to modelling excellence, and I got this in spades from my interviewees. I presented back my findings to my NLP group initially in August 2009 before starting to write the book.

One of the key learning points for me is that you've got to be a business person first and a coach second. When I started out, I wanted to be a great coach and didn't give a thought about what it took to be a business owner, or any of the other things I needed to grasp to get clients. But I also realised that I wasn't alone. The people I was interviewing had gone through some of the same things as me to a certain extent. Like Marian Way who said, "I spent a lot of time fiddling around with websites, as I didn't know what to do to start with. It took me a while to realise that it's not about sitting on your backside writing stuff on websites, it's about going out there, talking to people and networking."

Gladeana McMahon eloquently shared what it takes to run a successful business: "It takes drive, enthusiasm, determination, self-discipline, knowledge and business knowledge. You may only be one person but you still need to know how to make sure you are financially sound and how to do bookkeeping and administration, as well as knowing enough about marketing. A self-employed person is like a GP. In that if you think about a GP, they can turn their hand to most things in terms of diagnosis, understanding, and then refer to a consultant when it gets above a certain level."

What it also helped me to realise was that it was time to take my business to that next level. At the time of writing my first book I was in the process of negotiating reduced hours at work to allow me a better balance between my work and the business, and this is something from Blaire Palmer that resonated with me:

"People often provide too much of a cushion, they wait for redundancy, then they have a nice big redundancy payment and then there is no pressure to make the business work for the first two years as they have money. Then two years down the line they don't have the confidence to make it work because they haven't made it work already. When the money runs out they get a job. Then they will try and work part time but if the worst comes to the worst, they know they can increase their hours. Or they really reduce their overheads so they don't have to earn much money or their husband or wife supports them, so now there is enough money so they don't have the motivation to make the business work. Most people need some sort of rocket up them to make it happen. If you are not desperate and don't need it enough, you can't do the difficult things like go to the networking event, ask for the sale or charge enough."

Marketing was something that I'd studied at college, but I'd never applied it to the real world until I'd started my own business, and this was one of the reasons why I worked with a business coach. However, something that Michael Neill said to me made it seem easier: "You don't need 50 clients – you need one client. And when you've got that client, you don't need 49 clients – you need one client. And unless you are someone who is trying to create global domination instead of a successful coaching practice, it really is that simple."

This type of message takes the pressure off, doesn't it? It's difficult enough stepping up and doing much of the business stuff, and being able to take it one step at a time certainly felt more manageable. I wasn't looking for global domination (or at least not overnight anyway!) and it helped me to realise the steps that I needed to take to grow my business and also how I could sequence this information in a book to help others in a similar situation.

Ultimately there is an important message when you are in business, and it is that people don't buy what you do, as I mentioned earlier. They don't buy coaching, hypnotherapy, reiki or healing; they buy the result of working with you. Or as Hannah said to me: "They don't want to know about the techniques, they just want you to do them. You don't ask a surgeon where they trained and everything like that, you just trust yourself and you trust that they know what they are doing and they will tell you what they need to do at a certain time and get on with it."

The second most important message from these interviews was all around mindset, and most importantly, having the mindset for success. Well this was the reason for my modelling project, after all!

Unless you believe in yourself and what you are doing, how are you going to be successful? This was a key turning point for me as I understood the business concepts, although it wasn't until I finished writing the book that I realised how pivotal this was for me.

The difference that makes the difference

The mindset concept is incredibly important as it was something that I'd struggled with during the early stages of running my business. Being that mouse had impacted on how much I believed in myself and what I could achieve.

This congruency between who you are and what you project is incredibly important. Steve Marriott said to me: "If you are not confident in your ability to get people to their outcomes as a coach then you are limiting your chances of success because you're not allowing people to be confident in you. One critical factor is 'state leads state', and if you go in with a wobble or uncertainty then you're just not allowing your client to have any confidence in you. There has to be a degree of confidence to find the right question. Coaching isn't an exact science; you might ask three questions when you could ask one question, but when you find the right question that's great – like hitting the 'sweet spot' on a racket. You can take this person to a different place in their life."

You could also take on board what Allison said: "You have to walk your talk and you have to believe in what it is that you are doing so that other people can see that it is a genuine, authentic you. This belief has to be so strong; if you aren't able to talk about your product or service with 100% certainty then how can you expect your prospects to believe in you?"

One of the discussions I had with a couple of my interviewees was around the concept of fraud or 'imposter syndrome'. If you've never heard of this term, it means that you feel that you're not good enough, aren't successful enough, and that you will be 'found out'. There is something stopping you from truly believing in yourself, and you're more likely to do the next training course or qualification, rather than believing that you have enough resources already. Like many people, I'd experienced this concept numerous times throughout my life.

Interestingly enough, I later found out that up to 70% of people feel that they will be labelled as a phoney at some stage during their life so it is particularly common – and an experience I've gone through too. Reassuringly, though, I realised I wasn't alone when I interviewed my 'models'. One comment from Blaire really helped me hugely.

She said: "To get in the right frame of mind comes from experience. Coaching people one-to-one is a huge advantage as you get to see the squishy insides of those very high-up people. If these people are like that, probably everyone is like that. They might seem 'crunchy' on the outside, but most of us have fears and all of that on the inside. 'Fraud syndrome' is found the world over. If there is a name for it, a lot of people must be feeling it. The privilege of seeing those squishy insides of people is very reassuring and you have to trust you come across better than you think."

Shy girl tip – Why you are brilliant

Imposter syndrome is something that's come up for many of my clients, so I thought it was important to give you a tip if you ever feel like 70% of the population!

The first thing I'd like you to think about is this:

If you feel like a fraud, what proof have you got that this is so?

Whenever you feel this way, ask yourself for all of the counter evidence that shows why you are brilliant at what you do.

Everyone has a wobble from time to time that might stop them from doing what they really want. Sometimes it's worth taking time out to reassess where you are, and at other times it's about biting the bullet and doing it anyway.

The difference that makes the difference

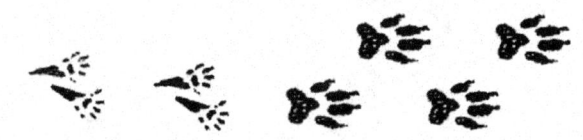

The mouse that roars

Chapter 12
How to write a book

I went on to write my first book. Writing a book isn't an easy thing to do and I struggled the first time around as I didn't know where to start.

The interviews were transcribed and I took the most important points and created a structure for the book. As I mentioned earlier, this eventually became *The Secrets of Successful Coaches*, a title that was agreed after a short poll with a few of my trusted business colleagues. I remember using flipchart paper and hundreds of coloured sticky notes to make sense of what I had learnt.

There were certainly key themes that my 'models' taught me during our time together. Some of the ideas were similar and others wildly different. It led me to realise that there is no one size fits all, a concept that I appreciated more later on in my journey.

Although I'd written a book before (but as I'd never been happy with it, it became an eternal

Word document), this time I knew I had to get it published. This was a minefield and I'll say in retrospect that writing the book is the easy part!

Being a lifelong learner, I started to explore the world of writing, publishing and promotion and studied some of the work produced in this field. I bought a copy of *The Writers' and Artists' Yearbook*, created a one page synopsis of my book, and started to approach some publishers. Yet writing a niche book had its advantages and drawbacks; one was that it was more likely to appeal to my intended reader, but on the negative side, it was never going to sell thousands of copies. In the end, I decided to approach a company who specialised in partnership publishing, although just as I signed the contract I had interest from a traditional publisher. But I chose the former option as I didn't want to wait any longer to get my book out into the world!

It had taken me a long time to write the book: over 18 months from conception to my book launch. This was partially down to inexperience, and it took a long time to get to grips with the messages too. Plus I went through three months of doubt. Like many authors I asked myself, "Who am I to write a book?", "Is it good enough?" and "Who's going to read it?".

How to write a book

I started to imagine I was one of my clients and I started to ask myself, "What evidence have I got for that?" and eventually I finished writing the book. Although if it wasn't for the experts who had willingly given me their time, I may well have binned my manuscript and done nothing with it!

I later learnt that it's OK to be worried in this type of situation, and that fear and anxiety is never going to go away. Hey, I'd walked on hot coals, so what would stop me from publishing a book? When you make the decision to stand out in this way and put your head above the parapet, you are opening yourself up to criticism; there will be people who don't like your work, but if you don't do it, how would you feel then? This has been one of the defining thoughts throughout my experiences and it helped the mouse to learn how to roar. It also now helps me to support my clients, many of whom are making equally scary decisions.

You don't know what's going to happen in the future, but don't worry about the few people who won't like what you do, as you will reach hundreds and thousands of people who will love you, and will learn from you, where you know you can make a difference. This is what spurred me on. One of my mentors once told me that when you start p**sing people off, then you know you've made it!

It has been said that children only have two fears when they are born, a fear of falling and a fear of loud noises, so this indicates that most of the fears that we face are learnt from our influences – family, peers and friends, as well as media and other sources – as we progress on our way through life. So we have a choice: whether to embrace these fears or do something else instead. I chose the latter!

I'd like you to believe that you can make a difference in this world. It takes one simple act of kindness to make someone's day, a smile that can change a person's view of the world, and a thought that brightens up a life. Even the little things can have a huge impact, creating a ripple effect, and just imagine what would happen if you decided to make these little things even bigger! Alongside the writing, I was working part time by then. Luckily I had a manager who supported me every step of the way – I even coached her for a time! I was developing my business, and doing what I love – helping people. I was getting brilliant results and great testimonials, but I had no serious plan to grow my business. Although I had a business plan of sorts – a high level document that didn't say much as I never kept it updated or reviewed it! I had a dream to give up my day job completely, but in reality no idea how to make it happen.

This reminds me of a critical message that I learnt from interviewing Hannah McNamara for my first book. She reminded me of the importance of a plan: "You've got to have a plan. Even if it's on the back of an envelope, you've got to know where you are going and what you're going to do to get there. It doesn't have to be something big; it can be a one-pager that's stuck on your wall or something. It could be a mind map. Within having a business plan is knowing your market, knowing your product, and knowing your pricing, what you are going to do with your product; that's all in the plan."

This was one of my drivers at that stage to do something different. I implemented what I was taught by my experts: I started to get clearer on my clients, and I began to make the transition to working with small business owners (predominantly coaches who were where I was when I started out in business).

I created my first online programme, I had a regular slot on the local radio station and built relationships with my local newspaper. I developed my first membership club, ran events, began speaking, and did a lot of things to get myself noticed. I also joined my first Mastermind group which was run by my business coach, and it was the first time that I'd seriously worked on growing my business.

I became smarter when I took Duncan Brodie's advice to concentrate specifically on three strands of marketing, so I decided to focus on networking, speaking and writing for the next couple of years, which certainly helped my business to build. That's not to say (with hindsight) that everything I did was the right thing, but I don't regret any of the experiences that I went through.

One of the things I found is that when you have a goal with a deadline, you're more likely to achieve it. If you say that you are going to do something within six months, it will always be that far away and move with you, but when you put a physical date on something it's more likely to happen by then.

Later that year, I decided to hand in my notice and leave my job. Actually in the end I felt I had no choice, as I wanted to take five weeks' holiday with my husband to travel around Australia (one of our dreams for many years), and I wasn't able to take all the holiday I needed to make it happen.

During the summer of 2010, I completed my first manuscript. I then employed a copy editor and left her with the book whilst I travelled halfway around the world. That was it. It was time to get serious about my business without the buffer of a regular wage. Although you could say that five weeks' travel wasn't the best start to going alone, but it's another thing that I didn't regret!

Shy girl tip – Overcoming doubt

At the times when you start to doubt yourself, there are a few strategies you can put into place.

- Learn to recognise thoughts that go through your mind, especially if they are negative.

- Challenge these thoughts and the basis on which they are made. Ask yourself, "What evidence have I got for the thought I am having?"

- Learn to make alternative explanations, challenge your thinking, and turn your negative thoughts around.

- Develop an excellent inner-voice to feel better about yourself and raise your self-esteem.

- Understand that our current views of ourselves are usually formed by a mixture of what we tell ourselves, what others tell us and what others say about us.

- Ultimately, adopt positive self-talk rather than focusing on the things that have gone wrong or the negativity you are facing.

- You might choose to use affirmations, such as one of my favourites 'I am enough' to help you to keep your self-talk positive.

Chapter 13
What the mind can conceive, it can achieve

Going to Australia wasn't actually part of my immediate plan, but travelling was part of my vision. It was one of those things that I really wanted to do and we had the impetus to make it a reality as you'll find out shortly.

That's why I believe that although having a plan is important, having a bigger vision of what this will give you is essential. When you have a vision, it gives you a focus and an aim to work towards. For me, it's always been more than having a list of things to do, a bucket list or even the intended New Year's resolutions. And when you are totally connected with this vision and why it's important, it makes the items on it easier to reach.

Napoleon Hill famously said, "Whatever the mind of man can conceive and believe, it can achieve", and you may think that having a vision board can also help you to manifest what you want. Although I do believe this up to a point, you've got to take action too.

The mouse that roars

For many years, I've started the new year with a vision board. I've taken a huge pile of magazines, a piece of A3 card, scissors and glue, and I've developed my aspirations through the medium of images and words. I develop my vision board in a holistic way and it encompasses all parts of my life, because ultimately everything in it is intrinsically linked. So travel is usually part of my plans when doing my vision board at the start of each year.

Perhaps the reason we love travelling so much is because Peter and I had never travelled extensively when we were younger. Peter went straight into a job and I went to college; it was later that I took my trip to Canada and left him behind. Regular trips abroad have always been an important part of our lives together, and suddenly we had the opportunity to create a holiday of a lifetime. As a result of him winning a competition with a first prize of £10,000, we decided to go for it!

Later people told us that what we saw during our trip Down Under, many Australians don't see during their lifetime. We worked with a travel specialist to put together an incredible journey. Starting in the vibrant city of Sydney, we were lucky enough to take in a stunning firework display during our stay. We saw the iconic sites like the Opera House, the Harbour

What the mind can conceive, it can achieve

Bridge, Sydney Tower, The Rocks, Bondi Beach and Manley, as well as Taronga Zoo with Darling Harbour in the background.

Hiring a car, we had a few days in the stunning Blue Mountains before flying to Cairns and taking a bumpy boat trip to the Great Barrier Reef. After the stormy waters of Port Douglas, we arrived in the serene blue waters of the Agincourt Reef, where I snorkelled for the first time – although admittedly letting go of the guide-rope was a different matter altogether. When our later helicopter ride showed sharks in the water, I did wonder why I did it! Next we flew to the north of the country to Darwin and the Kakadu National Park.

We had an incredible train ride on The Ghan to the Red Centre (although it was pretty green with all the rain that had fallen that year) and explored Uluru (aka Ayers Rock) and Kings Canyon among other attractions. This was one of the most mystical places on our journey with its raw beauty and ruggedness. Then we finally flew to Adelaide where we sailed over to the amazing Kangaroo Island and drove along the Great Ocean Road before arriving in Melbourne five weeks later. Phew. I'm exhausted just remembering it!

We managed to fit in a trip to see friends in Adelaide

and also met up with my very first paying client who had immigrated to the town with her daughter. It was great to catch up with her, and see how far we'd come, having both made different decisions in our lives for different reasons. She'd decided to escape the rat race and corporate world in the UK, whereas I was living one of my dreams of travelling around the world.

We also spent time with two lovely ladies on our trip; ironically they kept turning up when we didn't expect it to happen. After meeting them on a coach in the Northern Territory, they were then in the compartment next to us on the train, stayed in the adjacent apartment in the small village of Robe, and we finished our journey together in Melbourne without planning it to happen that way. We even bumped into them a couple of times there, despite it being a large city. It became a bit of a game; we'd expect them to be around the corner and there they were. We got on really well, shared similar values and enjoyed a meal or two together.

Travelling is a love of mine and I'll never say no to opportunities like this that are offered to me, and it's something that I love to fit in with my business. As the mouse, when it comes to having the courage to do something new, I'm willing to explore and do different things, but not without extensive planning first. I'm sure you can imagine that we wouldn't have fitted everything in if we hadn't planned it out meticulously first.

Shy girl tip – How to create a vision board

A vision or mood board helps you to visually create a picture of what you want your life to be like. When you know what you want and why it's important to you, this can help you to attract more of this. You may choose to create a vision board annually or have different vision boards for different parts of your life.

To help you to start to create your vision and goals, ask yourself these questions: What do you want to do, be or have this year? What are your goals, dreams or ideals?

1. Prepare to create your vision board. I like to take an A3 piece of card, a selection of my favourite magazines, glue, and scissors. Give yourself time and physical space to make this

happen. You may choose to put on some uplifting music too!

2. Taking your goals for the coming year, go through the magazines and cut out any pictures, words or phrases that resonate with you and your goals. Or you could print off some of your favourite quotes from your computer and use different materials and textures if you are feeling creative.

3. Once you have cut out your pictures, words, etc., arrange and stick them onto your board.

4. Place your board where you can see it every day to remind you of your goals.

5. Take action to get what you want!

Here are two final thoughts on creating a vision board:

- When you know what you want, you are more

What the mind can conceive, it can achieve

likely to attract this into your life. Of course, it's unlikely to drop into your lap unless you do something to make it happen, but at least you'll be taking action towards the thing that you really want to have.

- If you've got big dreams, break them down into manageable chunks. Otherwise they'll feel out of reach or as if you'll never actually achieve them. Simply look at the steps you need to take or people you need to call on to actually make them happen.

The mouse that roars

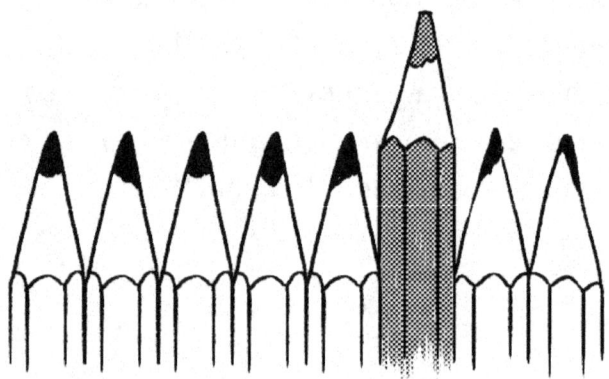

Chapter 14
It's time to stand out

Finishing the book once I returned from Australia wasn't easy. Even with a professional copy editor and proofreader, it's tough trying to get your book right. As an author, you get incredibly close to your material and it's not easy to see the errors, the pesky typos and the grammatical mistakes that need to be corrected.

Since the book had been a labour of love, I wanted to launch it in style and planned my book launch party for March 2011. It was a chance to celebrate with the people who had been involved in its creation and an opportunity to celebrate too. Also, giving myself a deadline meant I had no choice but to get the final edition ready to go!

I'll admit that it did feel pressured and rushed and I know I was a tad stressed, not only with the preparation for the launch, but also with the fact that I was about to do the whole 'standing out thing' in a big way. Reading through the journals I kept at this time, I can tell that my emotions were on a rollercoaster and I was struggling to keep on top of everything.

To support the launch, I was also doing new interviews with many of the people who I interviewed for the book. These were recorded and delivered as podcasts to create frenzy about the launch and to pre-sell the books before they were even printed. It was all about the buzz, something that I encourage my clients to do, as you don't need to wait until everything is absolutely perfect to get started with your marketing.

That reminds me of an important lesson that Allison Marlowe taught me, and that is 'imperfect action is better than no action at all'. I admit that I'm a recovering perfectionist, but I've learnt over the years that it is better to do something imperfectly rather than never actually get it done in the first place. On 4 March 2011, three weeks before my book launch, I'd been out with a friend (Jane Cooke, a brilliant personal stylist) who took me to Southampton to help me find the perfect outfit for the launch. It's said that when you feel good on the outside, it makes you feel good on the inside, and that's certainly something I'd been working towards!

It was on that same day that 200 books arrived in

It's time to stand out

my lounge. Although I was excited, I couldn't open the boxes because I was scared of what I might see inside. "Would I like them?", "What if there is a typo?"; all sorts of hesitations were going on in my head. But when I saw the final product, I loved what we'd created. Then 18 days later, I had my book launch.

I'm not one who enjoys attention, so making the decision to have a book launch was a scary one; but is there really any point in writing a book unless you decide to make an impact with it?

That's why just hours before the launch I was in a television studio in Portsmouth. Surrounded by cameras, lights and the bustle of people, I was interviewed about my book, another first for me, but a great chance to promote it. Then I was chauffeured by my husband to the hotel to meet my fans!!

The launch event was an experience that I'll never forget. We had a beautiful room with over 70 people in attendance, including four of the people whom I interviewed for the book, some of whom had travelled hundreds of miles to be there. Organised by my brilliant VA Tracy Harris, we had a photographer, cupcakes branded with my logo, and two inspiring speeches, one by Allison, and another by Roberta and

Wendy who did a double act. They said things that I would have never have even considered saying about myself, and then suddenly I was in the spotlight.

I'll admit that my presentation style has changed since then. Self-conscious with my first experience of speaking into a microphone, I've always had a tendency to blush when I'm unsure about myself or when I'm the centre of attention. But I was well prepared, so I gave my talk, shared some of the nuggets from the book and yes, I did it! I knew it was my evening to be in the limelight, and it was my choice, as much as I didn't enjoy it.

I took a huge leap out of my comfort zone to talk in front of everyone and the most startling thing was that they were all there for me. Fellow coaches, business owners, family and friends, I felt particularly cherished and supported that evening, and I know that I made my parents and husband proud. Even my grandma loved the book, although she didn't understand it!

One of the things that happened to me whilst I was preparing the talk had been a game changer and an unexpected 'aha' moment. I finally felt like a business owner first, and a coach second. I may not have been brave enough to call myself an entrepreneur at that stage, but I started to realise that I had some key skills that set me apart from my competitors, and that I had many tools in my toolkit to help them.

Following the book launch, I continued to step up in my business, even though there were times when it would have been easier to blend back into the crowd. I interviewed many more successful coaches for a follow-on audio series, including Nick Bolton, Kate Cobb, Nick Williams, Deepak Lodhia, Victoria Player, John Lees, Wendy Harrington, Nicola Bird, Maggie Currie, Topher Morrison, Viv Craske, Victoria Groom and Chris Matthews.

My Amazon launch took place a little later. 'A-Day' was 1 June 2011. Getting ready for an Amazon launch is a time consuming process. To be successful and get to the number one spot, the secret is to sell as many books as possible in a short period of time by offering incentives and bonuses, and getting people to support you.

I had many people sharing the information with their community and online, including my 'models', friends and fellow business owners. I do remember my excitement when I finally achieved the number one status in my category, and particularly recall taking screenshots when I was overtaking business greats such as Robert Kiyosaki's *Rich Dad Poor Dad* and *Influence: the Psychology of Persuasion* by Robert Cialdini. My long-awaited book was finally out there for all to read!

Shy girl tip – How to stand out

You don't have to be in business or write a book to stand out, so what can you do in your life to be more courageous, get noticed and become more visible?

This might be as simple as emphasising something that you're good at on your CV, telling people about a particular experience that you're proud of, or sharing your truth when you'd prefer to blend into the crowd.

It's time to stand out

The mouse that roars

Chapter 15
What if I had a year to live?

"I'm not scared of dying. I've always been of the philosophy that when your time's up, that's it. Am I scared of those close to me dying? Yes probably, but I think what scares me most is the thought of not living, not having the life that is amazing, satisfying and wonderful!"

This was my journal entry on 11 September 2011, particularly poignant as it came on the ten year anniversary of the 9/11 attacks in the United States. Since we'd stayed in the Marriott Hotel between the two twin towers in the late 1990s whilst I worked for the company, I had been affected hugely when I'd heard the news.

It was around this time that my good friend, Samantha Russell, introduced me to the book *A Year To Live* by Stephen Levine.

An American, Stephen spent much of his life caring for terminally ill cancer patients. He helped them to make the most of their last few months by running forgiveness and healing workshops and helped them to live and die more consciously. Then one day he thought to himself, why wait until you know that death is imminent before you live each day as if it was your last?

Armed with this newfound idea he and his wife, Ondrea, decided to embark on this adventure and live the next year of their life in this way. Subsequently he wrote a book about the strategies and techniques they used to live as if they only had one year left, and detailed their experiences in the book. It became a bestseller in 1998 and inspired followers all around the world.

So I read the book, understood the principles, and then a group of friends and myself took Stephen's challenge in 2012. We followed the philosophy behind the book for a year. It was certainly work in progress, and very challenging at times. It was an emotional and important year, and a very different experience for each of us.

Since I did the project, many people have asked me how it felt to live as if I had a year left. Some people have inferred that it would have been easy to spend all of my money during the year – and yes it would have been if I hadn't shown restraint!

But my approach was to treat each day as if it was my last to make the most of the experience and implement new habits and philosophies in my life.

Whenever I was offered an opportunity, every decision I made was borne of a conscious choice – "If I had a year to live, what decision would I take in this situation?"

Over the coming chapters, I'll share some of my experiences and learning from the year, and how it continued to help me to turn into the mouse that roars.

Shy girl tip – What would you do if you had a year to live?

This is a really tough question to answer, isn't it? I've known many people who have left this world too early, but on the other hand, if you don't ask this question whilst you're able to do something about your dreams, they might never happen.

Please give this question some thought, and in the meantime I suggest that you:

- Live every day as if it was your last. You don't know what's around the corner or what might happen tomorrow, so enjoy every moment and take advantage of every opportunity.

- Count your blessings, be grateful and forgive others who have wronged you. All very important concepts if you always want to approach your life as if you had a year to live.

What if I had a year to live

The mouse that roars

Chapter 16
My bucket list

I get really excited when I think about my bucket list. I see all the possibilities of things that I'd like to be, do and have and then sit down and think about it. My vision board has on it pictures of the places I want to go, the things I'd love to have in my life and the actions I'd like to take.

Taken from the phrase *kick the bucket* meaning *to die*, a bucket list is simply a list of things that you've not done before but want to do before you die.

The phrase was popularised by the 2007 film of the same name starring Morgan Freeman and Jack Nicholson. The plot follows the last few months of two terminally ill men who, after meeting in hospital, decide to take a road trip with their wish list of what they want to do before they kick the bucket. From doing a skydive to visiting the Taj Mahal, and riding motorcycles on the Great Wall of China, with inevitable ups and downs they make the most of their final months.

The mouse that roars

Many books have been written on this very subject, including *1,000 Places to See Before You Die* by Patricia Schultz. If you search for the term 'bucket list' on the internet, you'll get almost 19 million results, so it is a very popular subject. You'll also find some very poignant bucket list blogs from those who know that they haven't got long left to live, as well as people who have already passed away at a young age.

Of course, where you are in your life will determine how important your bucket list is, although when you know what you want to do, it makes it easier to tick a couple of things off each year, and make decisions based upon this list.

According to research in 2013 by funeral directors CPJ Field & Co, who were commissioned to identify the life ambitions of Britain's population, 20 million (42%) people have either already prepared their bucket list or are planning to write one. Ironically this is apparently many more people than have prepared wills! Not surprisingly, the top item on most people's bucket lists is world travel.

One other resource I found whilst doing

My bucket list

research on this subject was published in *The Guardian* on 26 September 2012. Kira Cochrane asks: *Bucket lists, are they a good idea?* in her article. She starts by saying: "Skydiving and swimming with dolphins are just two popular items on the lists of things people want to do before it's too late. But are they facing up to death – or merely in denial?"

She goes on to talk about John Goddard who at 15 created his own bucket list of 127 life changing and challenging goals, including running a five minute mile and climbing Mount Everest. Known as 'The World's Greatest Goal Achiever', his list has developed extensively, been achieved, and has been well documented. Mr Goddard's story was included in the ever popular and highly recommended *Chicken Soup for the Soul* series of books.

The *year to live* project in 2012 wasn't just about ticking items off my bucket list, although I did do a few things that I'd been putting off for years which were on the 'I'll probably do it one day list'.

What's on your bucket list?

If you're thinking about writing a bucket list, these are some of the most popular items that are on people's bucket lists. During the year to live I decided to conquer my fears by tackling some of them!

Make a difference by volunteering, donating blood or taking part in a charity event

I started to give blood again; it didn't take much to go onto the Blood Donor website and register for the next local session, and since I did this I've given blood regularly every four months. I also signed up to do a charity event in 2013.

Learn a new sport/new language/musical instrument

I decided to go skiing. This was a big thing for me, as my husband has been skiing since he was a child and my only experience had been a disastrous lesson in Whistler in 1997.

Visit a new country or a famous landmark/ one (or all) of the 'Wonders of the World'

For this you'll need to read on for my charity expedition that took place in 2013!

Set foot in each of the seven continents of the world

Although I didn't achieve this in that year, I started to get clients in all continents of the world! Having said that, I had already travelled to North America, Asia, Africa, Australasia, (with South America to come) and live in Europe. Just Antarctica to go!

Do a skydive/bungee jump/ride in a hot air balloon/go white-water rafting

Oh yes, I jumped out of a plane during 2012! And I have done a hot air balloon ride twice before in the States and Egypt.

Swim with dolphins/sharks

Although I didn't have time to swim with them, during our holiday to Florida in December 2012, I got to play with dolphins in their natural habitat in the Florida Keys.

Take up yoga, tai chi, or learn to meditate

I focused on mindfulness and meditation during the year and took up yoga for a time.

Write a book, screenplay, get on TV or be featured in a magazine

I wrote and published my second book and I ran my first conference, and I'd appeared on local TV twice previously.

Read a book or learn a new skill

I became a firewalk instructor!

My bucket list

Of course there were others that are still work in progress or that I'd achieved already. Things like taking up a new hobby or craft, meeting someone inspirational or famous, building your ideal home, going to a renowned event or show and eating in one of the world's best restaurants... But there's always time for these another day!

I also decided at that stage to write this book, which initially was focused on the *year to live* topic and I started to blog about each chapter as I went. Although it evolved in the meantime, I was approached by Money Supermarket who found my blog site. They suggested that I write a blog post for their 'Bucket list competition' and I won the runner up prize of £50!

Shy girl tip – Create your bucket list

Take a moment to write your bucket list. What experiences do you want to have in your life? Where do you want to go? What do you want to do? What's important to you?

Another great tip is to look at what you've achieved already and the term I love for this is creating a 'reverse bucket list'. I did this on the eve of my fortieth birthday when I sat down and wrote down everything that I'd accomplished already in my life. A very empowering and insightful experience!

Chapter 17
Doing the things that scare you

Like many people, I've had a tendency to put things off, at least in the past. Brian Tracy calls this Someday Isle, an idyllic holiday resort. Like many small resorts, it has its own culture, language and beliefs. The types of things that are said on this isle are: "Someday I will grow my business...", "Someday I will follow my dreams..." and "Someday I will give up my day job ..."

It may feel safe to be on Someday Isle, but if you are there yourself, are you really achieving what you want right now? During my *year to live*, I chose to move from Someday Isle.

I embarked on many things that scared me. It started in the March when I went skiing properly for the first time. I'll admit that I'm not very good, as I'm a very cautious skier; I like to stay in control and I don't enjoy taking risks. I think I fell within the first five minutes and I came last in the ski race on the final day.

There were times, though, when I wanted to give up. Like on the day when it was snowing heavily and was so foggy that we could hardly see a few feet in front of us – a pretty scary place to be. I also felt muscles I didn't know I had, that ached so much that sometimes I struggled to get out of bed in the morning. There were lots of bruises, plenty of falls, and a few disastrous moments (it's not easy putting a contact lens back in your eye when you are halfway up a mountain!).

But I must have enjoyed it, because I've been skiing every year since then. There is something special about being in the mountains: the fresh air, the beautiful scenery. It helps that we go with a brilliant group of people, and it is a great moment when you take off your ski boots and chill out, taking advantage of après ski time! I tried curling for the first time, there was schnapps tasting, I ate and drank too much, but importantly I got off the treadmill of everyday life – something I'm not very good at doing.

Doing the things that scare you

When I got back, I started planning my first conference for the November (the Star Biz conference) and I wanted it to be different. I asked a friend of mine, James Hunt, to organise and run a firewalk for me, and he suggested that I became a firewalk instructor. I laughed at first, but my promise to the *year to live* prevailed, and in May 2012 I found myself in Peterborough taking part in the four day course.

Doing something like this was more than training to help people to walk on hot coals; it was a transformational experience. I put myself through experiences I'd never dreamt of doing.

Looking back at my journal I went with a positive intention to play full out, trust, enjoy myself, make new friends and have a good time. And I did.

We started with goal setting and a good old board break (breaking a pine board with your bare hand) before doing our first firewalk on the first evening. When you do a firewalk, the most important thing is to get into the right state, something that I struggled with that day. Your energy needs to be high, your mindset positive and you need to be in what's called a peak state. It was probably more difficult as I'd done it before. Also this may have been because we had designed the fire bed as a team, set it alight, and I knew from the fan of flames that the coals would be pretty hot! Whatever it was, the implications of what I was really doing hit me that day.

They were long days, with the second day consisting of low rope and team building exercises, including a trust fall, where you lean backwards off a tall ledge (about five foot in the air) and trust that your peers are going to catch you. I almost ducked out of this one as it scared me. The first time I walked up the steps to the ledge where I had to lean back and let go, I decided not to do it. But I didn't want to miss out on this opportunity and tried again. Once I'd done it and my peers had indeed caught me, I was remarkably overwhelmed and emotional as I'd had the confidence to let go and trust. That was a huge step, as there were certainly times when I lacked trust, trust in myself and my abilities.

The weekend went on with preparing the glass for our glasswalk, breathing and meditation, bending metal bars with our necks, breaking bricks with our hands, an arrow break (breaking it with our neck against a solid wall), the glasswalk (which was incredibly empowering), and the 108 on the final evening. 108 firewalks on burning hot coals ... certainly an experience! During the weekend, despite moments of weakness and fragility, I started to discover my power, and learned to roar a little louder. I got back in touch with who I was and why that was important, and felt peace, relaxation and energy despite little sleep.

The next big challenge that year was a skydive. I was running an event in the spring of 2012 and I announced to the attendees that I was planning on doing a tandem parachute jump. I asked if any of them would like to join me and three of them put their hands up! This was the incentive to make me commit to it. On 1 September 2012, the five of us, Corrine Thomas, Emma Weatherstone, Sousa Hari, plus my husband and I jumped out of a perfectly good plane!

I should point out here that I am scared of heights! To actually get me up in the plane took a visit to a friend, Joanne Reeves-Baker, a hypnotherapist who helped me to get ready for the experience. But jumping out of a plane had been on my bucket list for so long and I had to make it happen. Plus it was a great opportunity to start raising money for charity.

By the time we'd reached Old Sarum, just outside of Salisbury, I was ready. I knew it was a once in a lifetime chance to do something awesome so I'm glad the weather held out for us, otherwise I could have easily bottled out of the experience. My philosophy is if my time is up, it's up, so I was going to do the jump anyway.

I don't like waiting around for things like this as I start to get nervous! Luckily it wasn't long after our safety briefing that we went up in the plane, but I know that none of us were ready for it. We donned our sexy blue jumpsuits and helmets, and met our instructors (mine was a mad South African named George). It wasn't long before we were on the rickety plane, taking off and flying over the patchwork of fields high above Wiltshire. It was certainly cosy on the plane and halfway up I sat on my instructor's lap being tightly strapped to him ready for the tandem jump.

It's hard to put into words how I felt. Deep inside I knew I had the resources to do it and I had put many of these into place, especially since I'd done over 100 firewalks just a few months prior to this. I matched my breathing to George's, calm and composed. Well at least I was, until suddenly the door was pulled up and we were the first couple out of the plane.

Sitting on the edge of the plane at 15,000 feet,

ready to jump out, was breathtaking. I was dangling there for a few seconds, with my legs back and head back, and then suddenly with one gentle push, whoosh, I was out. At that stage, there's no going back or turning around. Then we were free-falling for about a minute (although it felt like longer). I'm sure I swore or screamed, I don't remember which, but that rush of air and adrenaline certainly hit me quickly. Words cannot describe how it feels when you're free-falling through the sky at 140 miles per hour. It's noisy, scary, and awe inspiring all at the same time.

Then after this endless minute, George pulled the strap to open the parachute, and we shot upwards and I could feel the straps of the harness burning my thighs – but I was more pleased that it had opened! I was responsible for steering us for a few moments as George released the straps but it wasn't as nerve-wracking as I thought it might be. I'd love to say that I admired the view, but I think I was happier when I saw the landing zone below, which looked like a model village. It didn't seem real and it wasn't long before my legs were up for landing. As I sat on the ground, my legs were like jelly and it took a while before I was able to stand by myself.

Was it scary? Maybe a little! But what I

noticed about the whole day was the huge sensory overload and adrenaline rush. The next 30 minutes were full of emotions and as I was unable to eat before the jump, I needed to eat, drink and use the loo very quickly!

It was one of those things that, if asked if I'd do it again, I'd probably say no, but I loved it anyway. Also between us, we raised thousands of pounds for our charities. This was one of my intentions personally, because I'd also signed up to walk the Inca Trail to Machu Picchu in Peru in 2013, and this was a great way to start the fundraising.

From a business point of view, in this year I also wrote my second book, *How to Stand Out in Your Business*. Writing a book was much easier the second time around. As well as the fact that I'd made the mistakes and learnt from my experiences, I ran a group programme where I taught my new Seven Step Success System, and wrote the book at the same time. It took me just six months from start to finish. This book was different from the first as it was my own stuff; it was now time for me to step up and teach my wisdom to my clients.

This led me on to the last thing that I did that year which scared me, and that was putting on my first conference. The one with the firewalk. I had booked seven other speakers as well as me, which had been equally nerve-wracking to organise, as they were all people I admired. Plus a magic show on the Saturday evening, a charity book auction, and the firewalk. Well, I don't do things by halves!

Although my friend James Hunt ran the actual firewalk for me (with Kate and Taryn whom I'd trained with earlier in the year), I got people ready for the experience by raising their energy, working on their mindset and changing their state. The weekend went well, except the smoke set off the hotel's fire detectors!

Shy girl tip – Do what you'd love to do

You don't have to jump out of a plane or any of these other mad things to do the things that scare you, but what would you love to do that you've not yet experienced?

Write it down and then go and do it!

If you know that you've been putting off doing something that is important to you, get clear on how you can actually make it happen, and who needs to help you to do this.

Doing the things that scare you

The mouse that roars

Chapter 18
Living in the moment, forgiving and being grateful

The *year to live* project wasn't just about achieving things on my bucket list; that was just part of the experience. Our group had monthly calls and a few meetings during the year and we each had different things that we wanted to get from the programme.

One of the themes in Stephen Levine's book was mindfulness and meditation. I'm sure that if you were living your final months, you'd want to live in the moment, but how many people actually do this on a regular basis? We generally reminisce about the past, worry about the future and never truly take time to be.

With the pace of life becoming quicker every day, it is all too easy to rush through life, not really taking the time to be in the moment and stop. Think about the number of times you've been on a journey and reached your destination without being aware of how you got there. I know that's happened to me. Or perhaps you find

The mouse that roars

that there are times where you eat a meal without taking time to savour the food that is on your plate?

Living your life on autopilot doesn't allow you to be at your best every day, to notice what you enjoy, what you appreciate and what is good about your life. The mind and the body are implicitly linked and have a huge effect on each other. When you are consciously living every day, you can be present. Plus you can be aware of any niggles and frustrations and take action to deal with them. You can work out what you want to be different and do something about it.

I'll admit that I don't find it easy to do this and when I meditate, my mind often wanders when I'm trying to switch it off. Although during the year, I consciously took time to focus on this. It's also occasionally difficult to find the time. But I'll never forget a quote I once heard.

Apparently the Dalai Lama was asked by a reporter, "How are you able to fit in daily meditation when you have such a busy schedule?" The Dalai Lama smiled and replied that on normal days he meditates for one hour in the morning, and on extremely busy days he meditates for two hours. Contradictory, you may think. But meditation can centre you, allowing you to be more efficient and effective in your life and work.

After a short course in hypnosis many years ago, in the right circumstances I can take myself into a trance. It helps me to become more present, opening up my consciousness. I also know that when I am relaxed, I pay greater attention to what's happening in my life and respond to challenges and difficulties in a more rational, calm and composed manner.

One of the other parts of the programme was all about forgiveness. This had never been a topic that had entered my consciousness before that point, although by working through the book I soon realised that I could forgive myself for some of the things I'd done in my past and some of the ways in which I sabotaged myself. One of the ladies in our group wanted to forgive a family member. Part of her journey was focusing on how to let go of the past, eliminating resentment, attempting reconciliation with support from an outside organisation, feeling compassion for the other person, and being able to let go.

The things that I chose to forgive or release were the situations and experiences during my childhood that didn't serve me. There's not much point in dwelling on the difficult times in the past as they won't help me in the future. I embrace my life as it is now, with my quirks and shortcomings.

I let go of any negativity I felt towards things that were said to me at all stages in my life, and the feelings that were associated with those experiences. It's not to say that they didn't happen, as I've shared some of these with you in this book. But I also believe that things happen for a reason, even if it doesn't always feel like this at the time. Like the bullies who made me stronger, the comment at work that led to me setting up my business, and the feelings of fear, when I felt pretty invincible after I'd faced them. The hardship and difficulties I faced were no longer part of my future, and remained in the past.

I looked for a lesson rather than dwelling on the difficulties. I maintained perspective; what may be a flippant comment from someone else can take on a different meaning in your own mind, and it doesn't take much for the situation to spiral out of control when you don't let go.

Now that doesn't mean that you won't continue to come across similar situations in the future, but what it does mean is that you have the power to do something about it. If I feel negative or have feelings that are unhelpful, I like to find somewhere quiet and breathe in positive thoughts and breathe out negative emotions. Sometimes I'll write them down in my journal and then put a positive spin on what they really mean. You could also write them down and then throw them away, or carry out the physical act of putting the piece of paper in a balloon and letting it drift away.

I also took an attitude of gratitude. I've journaled for years anyway, and when I looked back at some of my writing whilst researching this book, I can clearly see the times in my life when I felt the most peaceful and grateful, and the times when I struggled. I took the time to seriously think about what I was really grateful for. I started looking for the life gifts that I received, the appreciation I experienced and the thankfulness that I felt. Like many people, I took so much for granted, and forgot to be truly thankful. I developed the habit of writing three things I was grateful for each day in my journal, and there were days when I struggled and others when I wrote a long list on my piece of paper.

It took me a while to recognise that being grateful is about appreciating the small things in life as well as the big things. For example, my husband making dinner, having clean sheets on the bed, or having time to do something that I enjoyed. There were other times when I was thankful for the big things, like getting a new client, meeting someone who inspired me, or it could also be something like narrowly avoiding a car accident or another horrible situation.

What I learnt is that facing the world with gratitude not only makes you feel happier, but creates a snowball effect. If you feel good about life, of course it will affect those around you too. Even if you're having one of those days when it feels like everything is going wrong and there isn't anything to be grateful for, you can dig deep and find those little things too.

During that year, I also carried out one of the suggestions in Stephen Levine's book: to write a letter to your loved ones. It was on the eve of my parachute jump (ironic, I know!) that I wrote a letter to my parents and my husband. The reason for doing this was that if something were to happen to me and I was unable to say my last goodbyes, I wanted to tell them how I really felt.

The letter I wrote was very emotional for me. I remember sitting at my desk amongst a soggy mess of tissues whilst I choked back the tears. I later told those important to me where to find the letter should the

Living in the moment, forgiving and being grateful

time ever come. But it's also important that this sort of thing doesn't replace telling people how you feel right now, rather than waiting for the inevitable to happen.

For me, the project was all about turning struggles into victories. So things I suggest to my clients now are: write a list of your successes, take a compliment rather than dismiss it, and don't take anything for granted. I believe it's important to take time to focus on what you want and what's gone right in your life, and let go of everything that doesn't go to plan. And life doesn't always go to plan.

Shy girl tip – Develop an attitude of gratitude

- Look for the lessons in every difficulty or challenge. Learn from your mistakes and work out how you can turn them into a win.

- Remember to embrace your life, be mindful, present and in the moment. Cherish every day, experience and find ways to remember them forever, because you never know when these memories will help you to get through a difficult experience.

- Keeping a journal is a great way to record your successes, the things you are grateful for, and turn negatives into positives every day to keep you on track. If you had to write down 3 things that you are grateful for today, what would they be?

Living in the moment, forgiving and being grateful

Chapter 19
Not having a year to live

It was midway through 2012 while I was talking about the project to my parents that my dad whispered to me, "What if I don't have a year to live?"

I remember it vividly, as it was just after he had been diagnosed with cancer for the second time. Ironically this wasn't long after he'd been given the ten year all-clear from the bowel cancer he'd had previously. This time it was different.

It was on 24 March 2012 that we realised that something was wrong. We were at his cousin's sixtieth birthday party when he started struggling to eat. He had a severe choking fit; it felt like something was stuck in his throat, and it was unlike my dad not to finish a roast dinner. Five days later he found out that he had a tumour in his throat, which was later diagnosed as oesophageal cancer.

When he'd had the bowel cancer, he'd had an operation to successfully remove the disease. This time the first port of call was chemotherapy. And he was sick, extremely sick. Since he'd been left with a smaller colon after the operation ten years earlier, this didn't help. He had three rounds of chemotherapy. He went with my mum to the local private hospital, which was friendlier and less sterile than the NHS hospital, to go through the rigmarole of receiving the chemical concoction that would kill his cancer cells. My mum would diligently sit with him each time he went into hospital, making sure that the cold cap which was designed to stop him from losing his hair stayed chilled, and looking after his every need.

After the chemotherapy, the tumour had shrunk, but the next stop was an operation to remove part of his oesophagus, and also to find out whether the cancer had spread. This date was 15 August 2012 and it was one of the worst days of our lives.

We knew it would be a long operation, and we were informed factually by the specialist that he had a 50/50 chance of surviving the procedure, which was a difficult statistic to take in. Mum and I took my dad to hospital and went home to wait for the news. We were told that we'd have a phone call by late afternoon, so when there was no news at 8pm, as you can imagine, my mum was climbing the walls. She was distraught, upset, and not sure what to do, so I took on the role of the carer, ignoring my own anxieties until we eventually got the news that he'd pulled through the operation.

There was a long road of recovery ahead; the effect of the chemotherapy and operation was tough on my dad. Sixty-eight at the time, he was ten years older than the last time he'd had cancer, and the effect of this second trauma was to age him incredibly. He struggled to move, to walk, and eating also became difficult. Since this experience, I've worked with a client who has been writing a book about nutrition and cancer and realise that the advice he was given was pretty poor, and I'm sure this didn't aid his recovery. But he struggled through and by the following April, he and Mum finally managed to book a holiday to Malta and had a chance to rebuild their lives again.

But during that trip to Malta, Dad started to feel unwell again. With hindsight, I'm sure he'd hidden his illness as he hadn't wanted to hamper the holiday or show how poorly he really felt – or perhaps he too wanted to make the most of every moment. He developed a cough, struggled to walk for long, and upon their return they were back to square one again.

A few days after they came back, my mum was so

worried that she called out a doctor in the middle of the night. And to her frustration, it took until morning for a locum to arrive, and even then he wasn't sure what to do. Eventually, he suggested that my dad visit the local hospital "just in case".

After a frantic call from my mum, we took Dad into hospital that morning. Hospitals are not a place that I enjoy; the clinical smell always makes me retch and I've been known on more than one occasion to pass out, even whilst being a visitor! You can imagine how frustrated we felt when, after taking Dad to the respiratory ward, they didn't find anything obviously wrong and were tempted to send him home. But my mum wasn't having any of it! She made sure that they kept him in hospital to do further tests based on his history. I remember Dad instructing her to "Remember what I'm wearing so that when I come out you'll bring me a clean shirt to match these trousers". But he never did leave the hospital, nor did he have that year to live.

Within a few days he was diagnosed with inoperable and incurable cancer which had spread all around his body. When he asked how long he had left, he was told that he wouldn't last the summer, and there were many times when we thought we were losing him. Those times when my mum got that call to come in immediately because he was struggling to breathe, and the moment when he was admitted to critical care just to keep him alive.

Five short weeks later he left us. But what that precious time did give us was a chance to reminisce, share old memories, and have precious time with my dad. I remember sitting by his bedside whilst he struggled to speak, didn't want to eat, and I can't even imagine what he was going through. We cried together, smiled through the tears, and it gave us time to say goodbye.

It also gave us a chance to prepare for his death and his funeral. We agreed that I would write and say his eulogy. We also decided on the pieces of music that he would like to have played at his cremation. We were able to respect his wishes and the lack of fuss that he would have wanted if he was there to see it for himself. We also agreed that instead of flowers, my dad wanted people to donate to the Rocky Appeal at the hospital (and we raised £800 for the charity, and were later invited to put a plaque on a memorial wall at the hospital).

Just before he passed away, I asked my dad that

difficult question: "What would you like me to say at your funeral?" I knew that it would be difficult, and I wanted it to raise a smile and share the essence of who my dad really was. And although I felt fearful, I knew it was something that I just had to do.

On Thursday 23 May 2013, I was called to the hospital as my dad wasn't expected to last the day. He had lost consciousness by the time I'd arrived, and we asked the chaplain to read him the last rites. I later found out that the psalm that she'd chosen to recite was the one that my parents had selected for their wedding some 42 years earlier.

Then at 3pm, my dad gently, quietly, and peacefully passed away with my mum and I by his side. He left the earth with one final sigh before the shell of his body was left behind, grey, ashen, devoid of any soul.

Nothing prepared Mum and I for Dad's death. At least when he'd had the operation the previous August, we knew it might happen, and he'd prepared my mum with all the passwords and everything she needed to know if his time was up. That was typical of my dad. But this time the five weeks had passed with a blur of hospital visits, and as he was just a month shy of his seventieth birthday, it wasn't really expected.

Not having a year to live

We had expected him to pull through just like he'd done before.

It wasn't an easy few weeks to get through. After 44 years with my dad, my mum was devastated. There were times when I didn't know how I was going to get through it myself as we arranged the funeral and I prepared my tribute.

I vaguely remember my aunt and uncle coming to stay to look after my mum, and the meetings with the funeral director and the clergy taking the service. It was a haze of emotions, feeling lost and not being sure what to do next. I threw my heart into preparing the right eulogy for the service, wondering if I'd do my dad justice.

Friday 7 June 2013 was the day of the funeral. I remember being taken to the crematorium by the black funeral limousine to see Dad's coffin ready to be taken in when we arrived, a reminder of why we were there. With over 100 people at the funeral – there was standing room only – when the time came, I took my spot at the front of the room. I took a deep breath, looked at all of the people who had come to celebrate my dad's life with us, and gave his eulogy.

Shy girl tip – Write your own eulogy

If you were writing the eulogy for your funeral, what would you want someone else to say about you?

I encourage you to write your own eulogy, outlining the turning points in your life, emphasising the highlights and sharing your memories. Then I encourage you to share these with people who care about you, and perhaps they can do the same.

Why don't you tell people what music you'd like to be played, what you'd like to have happen, and how you'd like people to remember you and your life?

Not having a year to live

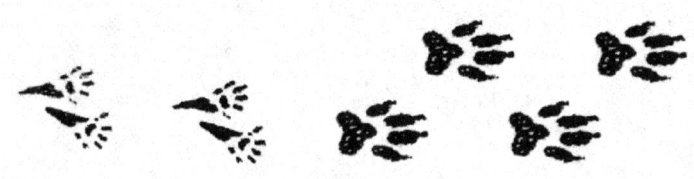

The mouse that roars

Chapter 20
Managing your mojo

There will be times when you just have to do something because the occasion demands it. But people will understand if you struggle, find it difficult or break down with emotion. Although it may feel counterintuitive, you've got to put yourself first. If you're always looking after others and putting their needs first, you'll find yourself struggling to do everything.

There were two things that I'd committed to doing during the *year to live* project: to run my second Star Biz conference in July 2013, and to raise £3,500 for the Genesis Research Trust, which culminated in a charity trek to Machu Picchu.

I was just about to start the promotion of the conference when my dad fell ill. I'd already publicised the date and started to create a buzz about the event, so it was a tough decision whether or not to go ahead. But I decided that I'd already committed to it; I'd found the perfect venue (a wine estate in Dorking) and this time I'd booked my friends, Kate and Taryn, to do a glasswalk, so I decided to proceed as planned. We also made it easier by making it a one day event, with just one speaker (me!).

In addition, I took the pressure off by getting some affiliates to support me, relied on my VA to get things done, and did my best to look after me – which I don't find very easy! I re-prioritised what was important and let a few things go. I still went to the Winning Women networking group in Cheshire where I'd previously been invited to speak and had a few days away to recharge my batteries too. But I no longer worried about numbers and filling the event, and trusted that the right people would be there.

So although there were times when I felt unready and ill-prepared, the conference took place in July 2013. I have always had a tendency to berate myself and this occasion was no different! But the event was well received, and the participants loved the glasswalk, which certainly made the day memorable.

I'll admit now that after the conference, I crumpled ... I was in tears at the meal with friends to celebrate after the event. The event had kept me going when everyone around me was struggling, and I kept them together. Suddenly, once

Managing your mojo

it was all done, I fell apart. I'd never really taken the time to grieve and I went through plenty of ups and downs during that period. But I never stopped. I kept plodding on, and as well as working I was also preparing for the charity trek. Over the summer, I spent a week walking the South Downs Way as part of my training (100 miles over seven days from Eastbourne to Winchester with my mother-in-law Judith and her friend John). But I can see now how much strain this put on me.

I've never found it easy to put myself first, and find it's easier to go with the flow and accept what will be, although now I see how hindsight is a magical thing!

In September 2013, I joined a group of 20 other amazing women to do the charity trek in Peru. Although I'd met some of them previously, we all convened in the early hours at the airport, and then three gruelling flights over two days got us to our final destination, Cusco, in Peru.

Now one of the problems with Cusco is the altitude. It's 3,400 metres above sea level, which means that many people experience problems with altitude sickness, which affects people in different ways. We had a couple of days to acclimatise before the trek, taking in a short walk around the city and a warm up trek to get used to the terrain.

Those around me were struggling, suffering from headaches and sickness, but I didn't feel too bad for the first 24 hours. Then the day before the trek, it hit me, but in a different way. I was unable to breathe, which was a bit of a problem. In addition, this made me feel anxious; my head was fuzzy and I couldn't concentrate. So it wasn't long before the trek's doctor was called. Within an hour I was admitted to the local hospital with suspected pulmonary oedema (which I later realised could result in death!).

The doctors at the clinic didn't mess around; I was sent straight to X-ray. After being taken by wheelchair to a private room, I had nurses paying me a lot of attention. I remember texting my husband trying to relay what was going on as he was trying to sort out the travel insurance, and in my hazy state, all I could say was "there are Spanish-speaking nurses doing stuff".

An elderly man came into my room, dressed in blue overalls and jeans, who I wrongly guessed was the maintenance man until he started taking blood from my right arm. And to my left was another nurse who was taking my temperature, taking more blood, giving me oxygen and a nebuliser, and fitting a cannula into my arm before giving me antibiotics and other medication.

Although the doctor spoke good English, most of my time was spent with the nurses and I hadn't studied Spanish for 20-plus years! It was an incredibly lonely 20 hours in the clinic, and as the trek was due to start at 6am the following morning, I didn't know whether I'd be stuck there or be able to join the rest of the team.

5am on the day of the trek was decision time. After more X-rays and with plenty of begging, the doctor allowed me to leave the clinic and do the trek. I wasn't well, but they hadn't found anything significantly wrong with me, and the treatment was beginning to help. On the plus side, when you begin the Inca Trail you start the trek from a lower altitude, so I started to feel a bit better. However when I look back on the four days now I realise that I was very poorly and went into survival mode to complete it. Despite training hard, I struggled to complete each day.

Nothing can really prepare you for this type of challenge. None of us knew how we were going to be affected – the long exhausting days, lack of sleep, high altitude of course, and the sheer scale of what we were undertaking at times. Steps, steps and more uneven steps! But you have to keep at it, breaking through some of your own barriers and taking that next step to get up and then down the mountain.

I wasn't the only one finding it tough, and even the fittest members of the group struggled with the elevation, lack of oxygen and the hard work of the climb.

I was inspired by the determination of the ladies on the trip, who were there for others when they needed their support. The level of camaraderie was amazing. Simple words of encouragement, a chance to let off steam, and a shoulder to cry on were all much needed over the four days!

Every day I had to take my trousers down to receive an injection in my bottom, as well as receiving intravenous antibiotics into the cannula that was still sticking out of my arm. My head was still hazy and the simplest things like putting together an outfit for the day were incredibly hard to do, despite the fact that I only had four T-shirts and two pairs of trousers with me!

Three nights of sleeping poorly in a tent pitched on uncomfortable ground took its toll too and for someone who likes her creature comforts, only having an inch of cold water to wash in, and toilets which were just a hole in the ground, didn't help me. Plus we had hail, snow and a landslide during the second night in the mountains too! But somehow I did the trek.

On the final morning, when we did our last push to Machu Picchu, the heavens opened which delayed our start. But finally we reached the Sun Gate, the first place where you should be able to see Machu Picchu in the distance. After an hour, the mists finally lifted and we saw the beautiful ruins below us. It was an incredibly moving experience, and one that I'll never forget, and made the previous four days of walking worth it. We eventually reached Machu Picchu, mixing with the clean people who had cheated and taken the trip by train!

We celebrated that evening, and being part of a group who raised over £96,000 for charity definitely made the pain worthwhile! Later, on 15 May 2014, we were recognised at a presentation in the House of Lords with the patron of the Genesis Research Trust charity, Lord Robert Winston, and had a few glasses of bubbly afterwards to celebrate!

Shy girl tip – Celebrate your successes

Too often in life people give themselves a hard time when things go wrong, yet forget to celebrate successes. In my experience, going through the hard times makes you stronger, as you can learn from these difficult times.

So here's my suggestion to you today. Congratulate yourself when you achieve something that's important to you: What reward do you need to give yourself when you've done it, however big or small?

Managing your mojo

The mouse that roars

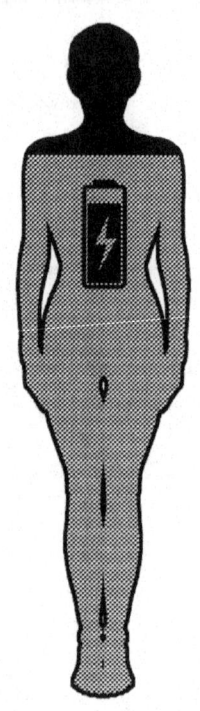

Chapter 21
Topping up my vitality bucket

At the end of the trek, we had one more night in Cusco before returning to the UK. Another night at high altitude resulted in more problems and I was in tears as we boarded the plane the next day, and I wasn't the only person suffering. But the last thing I wanted to do was remain in Peru, and I focused hard on returning to the UK. When I finally reached home three plane journeys later, my husband was sufficiently worried about me to take me to hospital the next morning.

With everything that had gone on in my life over the year previously, I'd never really taken time to look after me and manage my mojo. Although I was eventually given the all-clear, even at the hospital the nurse told me to rest for at least a week, and I had clients booked in on the Wednesday! But I did mostly heed her advice and rested apart from the one day. And although I felt able to work at my best on that day, this one exertion put me back days in my recovery.

The mouse that roars

I've always found it easy to say to my clients, if you don't look after you, how can you look after anyone else? And I'd missed that lesson myself. It was easier to get swept along, saying yes to every opportunity, always being busy, and not making enough time for me. If I wasn't at my best, how could I look after everyone else? Although I thought I was doing the right things, it wasn't long before I realised that I wasn't.

Those next few months weren't easy, although I didn't show it on the outside. I learnt the hard way that I needed to put on my own oxygen mask first before putting one on someone else. I started to learn how to be kind to myself and began to build myself up slowly.

I will always remember a talk I went to with life coach Alyssa Abbey, author of *Stop Making Excuses* and *Start Living with Energy*. Alyssa talks about our bodies being like a vitality vessel or bucket. When we live our lives we put in sleep, exercise, work, hobbies, etc, yet whatever we put into it, there are often leakages through holes in the bucket. These leakages are things like perfectionism, worry, frustration and fear, and unless we top up the vitality bucket, we are

Topping up my vitality bucket

going to struggle to have the energy to live our life the way we want. When you know what is leaking your energy this does, of course, allow you to plug the leaks and minimise the things that drain you.

So I started to top up my vitality bucket. I went to bed earlier and slept for longer. I looked at my nutrition levels, and remembered to drink green concoctions. In early January 2014, I did a seven day juice fast – which was tough, I must add! I continued to exercise, but slowly rather than doing day-long walks (as I was also recovering from a knee injury which I sustained on the trek). I spent time with people I cared about, and took more time out.

From a work point of view, I worked smarter. Although I'd started writing this book already, it was put on hold until I was able to give it the focus it needed to finish it. I developed my first ongoing information product (the Business Wow Factor membership) and ran a workshop and afternoon tea event in November 2013 to launch it.

I took more time to prioritise. I've always had a tendency to write a to do list, but this can also become overwhelming if you don't focus on which things on the list are the most important. Also if you don't plan how you're going to achieve it, will it happen? I know I can often plan to do more than I can actually realistically achieve in a day or a week. So I learnt that it was important to plan for reality, factor in interruptions and manage my workload better. I know the importance of breaking things into bite sized chunks, and I made sure that I heeded my own advice.

I also planned more and on a workshop with Emma Sargent and Tim Fearon later that year, I started to create a compelling vision for my life and my business, and how they could fit together to give me what I truly wanted in the first place. I saw what I wanted to create, why it was important to me, and then I started working out what needed to take place to actually turn this dream and ideal into reality.

Shy girl tip – Rate yourself

I often ask myself three questions that Steve Marriott taught me during our training a few years ago and I'd like you to do the same.

1. How is your energy today on a scale of 1–10, with 1 being feeling exhausted and 10 being the best you've ever felt?

2. How is your openness today on a scale of 1–10, with 1 being that you need convincing, and 10 being that you are excited about finding out new ideas?

3. How is your focus today on a scale of 1–10, with 1 being that your mind is elsewhere today and 10 being that you are fully focused on what you are here to do right now?

Then I'd ask yourself what needs to happen to raise each of these areas by one or two points.

The mouse that roars

Perhaps you need to ... stand in the garden with your bare feet and ground yourself, dance around the room to raise your energy whilst listening to your favourite music, go to the gym, go out for a walk ... or whatever makes you feel better

Chapter 22
Leaving a legacy

This book has taken me a while to write and has been in various states of undress and disarray. I felt that by sharing my story, I could inspire you to be one of those people who takes their life up a gear rather than letting it pass you by. One of my reasons for writing this book is to leave a legacy.

One of the turning points in getting this book finished happened in January 2014, although admittedly it resulted in a total rewrite. Still grieving after the death of my dad, my business had struggled because I was unwell and couldn't put the time and energy into it. But the new year was the incentive to get back on my feet. Then a very good friend suggested that I see a psychic medium. Although I'd call myself pretty spiritual, I'd never experienced this before, but I felt that I needed something – anything – to get back on the right path. Up until this point, only a handful of people have known about this (and I haven't even told my mum until now!).

Whether you believe this type of thing or not, this was one of the things that turned my life around. Although some of the things that she identified were obvious – as I spent much of the session in tears – she also told me things that she really couldn't have known.

She picked up on the fact that I grew up feeling isolated, and that people didn't understand me. She identified that I was feeling below par and run down, and that this was affecting my emotions. She saw that I had an inclination to overanalyse, and was a bit of a perfectionist. She identified my lack of courage and confidence and told me to believe in myself more.

There were things that she couldn't have picked up from me, which I found a little disconcerting. Things like the fact that I wasn't supposed to be called Karen when I was born, that my dad wanted to come back as a butterfly, that he had had problems with his speech towards the end of his life, and that I wrote and delivered the eulogy when he died.

She also asked me if I was writing a book about my

Leaving a legacy

life and when I confirmed this, she said that my dad wanted me to start writing again. Which I did, and I decided to dedicate this book to him.

My dad left a legacy to me through making a difference to my life and many others; this was evident by the number of people who were at his cremation. A legacy doesn't have to be a bequest in your will or a sum of money to charity – unless you wish – it can be the difference you make in the world and the memories you leave behind.

I've started to use my experiences as my legacy, which is I why I have written this book to share my story, and in May 2014, I started to tell more people about it. At the event *Speak like a TED Talker*, run by one of my favourite speakers, Sarah Lloyd-Hughes, I developed a talk called 'Are you ready to die?' This talk had a phenomenal response from my fellow speakers in the room.

I later shared the talk on my YouTube channel, but as the typically shy child, I was reluctant to share the video and could think of all sorts of reasons why not to share it – like the fact that it was recorded on a basic camcorder, the camerawork was a bit shaky and it wasn't perfect – but ultimately the message was more important than the excuses for not telling people about it.

In the nine minute talk, I tell my story interweaving the five regrets of the dying as originally researched by Bronnie Ware, an Australian palliative nurse working with terminally ill cancer patients, and documented in her book of the same name.

I'd like you to learn from some of my wisdom before it's too late, and take encouragement from me that you can live a richer life and leave a legacy. Through knowing my story, please take heed from some of the experiences that I've gone through and the strategies that I share with you. It doesn't matter whether you're a mouse or a lion, you can be your best to make a bigger difference.

Be inspired by others. I see well respected people in my field, some who are alive, and some who are dead, who have made a lasting impression. Just like the late Jim Rohn, the late Steve Jobs and inspirational entrepreneurs like Richard Branson.

But as I prove, you don't have to be someone famous or well known to make a difference. You can leave a legacy by impacting on one person at a time. Whether you get to know who you are by

Leaving a legacy

researching your family tree, raise money for charity, pay it forward by performing acts of kindness to strangers, inspire people through your work, or simply treat yourself and others well.

In the 1949 film, *It's a Wonderful Life*, the main character George Bailey gets the chance to do this. The film shares his story of being someone who has given his life to help others but doesn't see this. He questions his life and contemplates committing suicide. He is then saved by his guardian angel, Clarence, who shows him how life would have been different if he hadn't been born. It is a powerful message and it is worth considering these things – your most important moments and perhaps your biggest regrets.

Here are two questions for you to consider:

- **Who inspires you?**

- **What legacy do you want to leave?**

Shy girl tip – The rocking chair test

It's very easy to get caught up in the things you should, ought or must do rather than what you actually want to achieve. Start by defining what you want to achieve and why you want this. The how can come later.

Step 1 – What do you want?

I'd like you to start by taking yourself forward to your eightieth birthday (or any date that feels comfortable in your future). I'd like you to imagine your incredible life, what you have achieved, the amazing things you have done, the fantastic things you have seen, and the changes you have made in your life.

Then write down what you want. This process will help you set short, medium and long-term goals for your life. Devote ample thinking time to each stage.

Step 2 – Why do you want it?

Write in one brief sentence why you want to be, do or have each item on your list. If you can't do this with some of them, then cross them off.

You may find it easy to say "I don't want x" but what do you actually want instead? If you focus positively on what you do want to be different in your life, it makes it easier to concentrate on the tangible outcomes and benefits.

Step 3 – Start to prioritise

With your list in front of you, what are the most important things that you want to achieve and why? You might find it easier to divide your goals into ongoing goals which require regular input, short-term goals that you can achieve within a month, medium-term goals that may take between a month and a year, and longer-term goals that may take more than a year.

The mouse that roars

Take your top 10 goals – these are the ones you are going to work on – and make them specific, measurable and timebound and use these to start to create your personal action plan. Oh, and then take action!

Leaving a legacy

The mouse that roars

Chapter 23
The next steps in the journey

In the time between starting and finishing this book, I decided to write another one. During this period, I was still working with my clients who were generally coaches, therapists and other solo business owners in all corners of the globe, many of whom were starting out. I was speaking at events, running workshops and online programmes, and working one-to-one with my clients. As I continued to raise my profile and increase my visibility, people were recognising other things that I'd achieved.

Early in 2014, I had many people saying to me, "Karen, you've written a couple of books; how did you do it?" I realised that I had something important to say and my third book, *Your Book is the Hook*, was unleashed. Although I'd done some odd bits of work helping some of my clients to develop their books as part of their business development, it hadn't occurred to me that I needed to refocus my business until then, and that I'd found the thing that I loved to do.

Ironically I'd also neglected to follow some of my own advice. I'd written my second book *How to Stand Out in Your Business*, but I wasn't doing everything I suggested and standing out! Although I was getting great successes, I suddenly realised I was just another business coach, and something needed to change.

I started to model what I'd done for my previous books, understanding what I'd learnt (and also the mistakes I'd made) and looking at the step-by-step processes that I'd followed.

Writing *Your Book is the Hook* was easy. I like to try things out before I teach them to my clients so that I can find out what works and what doesn't. One of the things I decided to do was develop a group programme that I started marketing in August 2014 through a series of webinars. This programme was to take people through the six steps that I teach my clients to go from their idea to a published business or self-help book, with all the milestones in between including planning and writing the book, and the all-important marketing stage.

Dozens of people signed up for the course and some wanted to work with me on a one-to-one basis too.

The next steps in the journey

I also found that running the programme over a short period of time helped me to write 33,000 words in just five weeks alongside running it. I also decided to pre-sell my book, which created a buzz and helped me to attract new clients who were on a similar journey.

During that period I also ran my first writing retreat. One of my clients lived in Spain and we'd been talking for ages about running a retreat in her village. This took place in September 2014, and before I'd left I booked the next writing retreat for the same period in 2015, and I'm looking forward to many more in the future! Fittingly this is the place where I've been doing the final edits for this book, as well as helping my clients to get their ideas down on paper too.

It's a different pace of life in the Andalucían mountains – an amazing and beautiful environment, and on both occasions, my clients who joined me had a magical time to write. Being in a quiet and inspiring environment, it was the perfect location for getting on with writing a book. And of course, mentoring in shorts and a T-shirt by the pool is just the life I imagined when I started my business back in 2006, and part of my vision.

Business is so much easier when you

have a cohesive and consistent message. People get that I help them to write, publish and promote their book, and I give them the courage and freedom to do it. I also ensure that this book helps them to build their business, as I know the difference it can make to their business and their lives. This has been true for me too. I was told that my first book put me on the map, and I've developed it further by investing in my business, learning from others, rebranding, and I'm always stepping up to the next new and exciting challenge.

Ultimately walking my talk led to great PR for this book in the *Daily Express* before I'd even finished it, speaking engagements all around the UK, and I've even started my next book!

Ironically the driver I had when I started out, of wanting to make the difference and change the world, I'm able to influence more by helping my clients to get their books written. This enables them to reach more people through their wisdom and knowledge, and grow their business at the same time. By stepping up my clients have had articles published in magazines, are sought after speakers, and are standing out in their own unique areas of expertise, now that they know what this is and how valuable it is for others.

I've learnt over the years that you need to hear things more than once before you decide to take action or do something different. So listen out for those clues to what you really should be doing with your life. What you find easy is where other people struggle, something I always have to remind my clients! That's a great basis for a business and also a book :-)

Shy girl tip – Become the mouse that roars

I'd like to share 10 final thoughts.

1. Seize the day. Live every day as if it was your last and take advantage of every opportunity that presents itself to you. And if it doesn't, create new opportunities for yourself. Take time to live in the present and embrace every moment.

2. Be adventurous. You can do those things that are on your bucket list, or just bring a little challenge or adventure into your life to make

it more exciting. Stretch yourself and do those things that scare you.

3. Have some fun and laughter. Make a pact to smile, laugh and have fun every day. See the humour in difficult situations, do something joyful or even twist your mouth into something that resembles a smile!

4. Be kind and courteous. If you treat other people well, you are more likely to receive the same in return. So practise this in everything that you do – when you are driving, chatting to a friend, and especially when you are talking to yourself!

5. Be aware of your choices. You have a choice as to how you feel about a situation so make a choice to see the good. Stand for what you believe in, say how you feel, or do something about it. Life's too short to get frustrated when things go wrong.

6. Be positive and practise gratitude. Having a glass half-full, full or overflowing attitude is going

The next steps in the journey

to enhance your life. When you see the up side in every opportunity, it will make life happier and more fulfilling. That's not to say that things don't go wrong, but sometimes they happen for a reason.

7. Take time out. Going at full pelt every day isn't going to help anyone. Remember the Dalai Lama quote that I shared earlier. Taking time out will allow you to be more balanced, more in control and able to face challenges in a calmer and more measured way.

8. Look after you. Just to remind you, if you don't look after yourself, how can you look after anyone else? What do you need to do each day to be at your optimum? What new habits do you need to put into place?

9. Be with people who affirm and encourage you. The late Jim Rohn said that "You are the average of the five people you spend the most time with", so doesn't it make sense

to spend time with people who inspire and encourage you rather than people who are always holding you back?

10. Go for it! Go for your dreams, go for your goals, create new ideas, aim for that target. Never give up, overcome your obstacles and get what you want to create in your life!

The next steps in the journey

Epilogue – A letter to my older self

Dear Karen,

If I could give three pieces of advice to my older self, it would be these.

1. Just be yourself. Some people will like you, some won't, and that's OK.

2. Don't let the bullies win. It's OK to be different from others. Be unique; that's where you'll shine.

3. Live your life to your full potential, enjoy every moment and don't sweat the small stuff.

I'd like you to appreciate that life has its ups and downs, and you'll probably continue to make mistakes along the way. You'll probably sabotage yourself from time to time too.

Just continue to challenge yourself, take time out to have fun and remember, always, to top up your vitality vessel.

People have asked: What's happened to the mouse?

Funnily enough, she's still there. She'll always be there on some level, telling you it's easier to hide and squeak, rather than stand out. But what sort of life is that?

You've learnt that the trick is to know when to squeak and when to ignore the mouse, to use your tools and things you have learnt, and roar whenever you feel the moment is right for you.

Lots of love xxxx

About Karen Williams

As a business book mentor, I work with coaches, therapists, trainers and consultants who want to stand out from the crowd and write a book that helps them to grow their business. I help them to create and market their best book – the book that increases their confidence, raises their credibility and attracts higher-paying clients. I help them to overcome their fears, have the courage to share their best stuff, and ultimately change lives through their writing.

I am the author of four books: the Amazon number one bestseller *The Secrets of Successful Coaches*, *How to Stand Out in Your Business*, *Your Book is the Hook*, and *The Mouse That Roars*. As well as helping my clients to publish their own books, I have contributed to five other business books, speak at business events and run my own writing retreats and workshops.

This book is a personal project that I have known

that I've needed to write for many years, and I hope that it inspires you to live your best life. I live in Hampshire, UK with my husband and we both love to travel and enjoy our lives.

Connect with Karen

Thank you for reading this book and I would love to hear how it has inspired you. You can leave a review on Amazon or feel free to contact me direct.

You can find out more about my business and my books at my websites **www.selfdiscoverycoaching.co.uk** and **www.librotas.com**, and feel free to connect with me via social media.

Of course, if you'd like me to support you with your business and your book, just drop me a line!

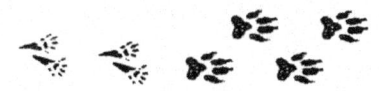

www.ingramcontent.com/pod-product-compliance
Lightning Source LLC
Chambersburg PA
CBHW071431080526
44587CB00014B/1804